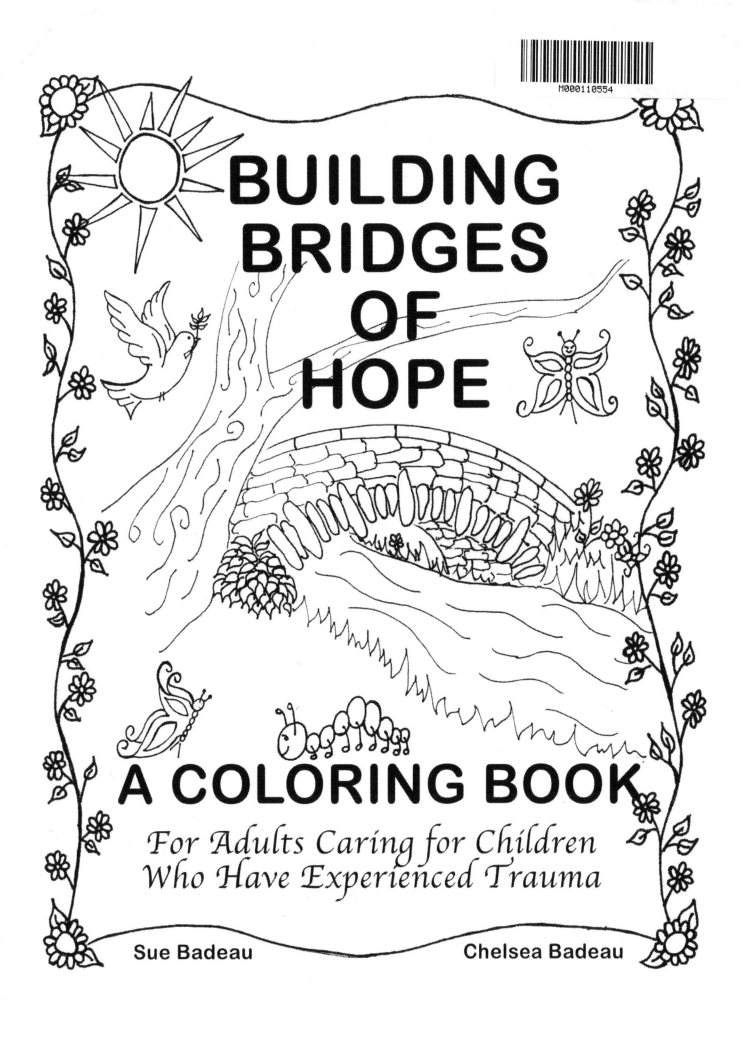

What People Are Saying About This Coloring Book

When an author/trainer walks the walk and talks the talk, has experienced the joys of life and the pain of death and goes forward to share those life experiences with heart, soul and a brilliant mind, you know you are learning from a master. That has been my experience with all that Sue shares. Enjoy her simple measures to heal the spirit with this latest masterpiece and be prepared to relax while you learn! **Bette Hoxie, Executive Director of Adoptive and Foster Families of Maine and the Kinship Program**

Relaxation strategies don't have to be work. Using Coloring and other calming techniques, Sue Badeau captures some of the key points to regulation in a fun and practical way. **Mary M. McGowan, Executive Director of ATTACh**

My dear friend and colleague, Sue Badeau, an internationally known author and expert on trauma has long been training on the value of mind/body/spirit connection in coping with stress and healing trauma for children and adults. I am thrilled to see her new book. In step with today's trend of coloring books for adults, "Building Bridges of Hope" is filled with tips, tools and strategies that Sue has been developing for many years (far ahead of the "trend"). Sue's talented daughter, Chelsea, created the beautiful images, including butterflies, bridges, and flowers to capture the concepts of calm, safety and connection. This coloring book is a wonderful tool to use with youth and adults who have experienced trauma in their lives, as well as those seeking greater mind/body/spirit connection. **Lisa D. Maynard, LMSW, ACSW, RYT, Certified Trauma Sensitive Yoga Teacher**

Sue has a special talent for presenting complex information in ways that are easily grasped. She helps us understand the effects of trauma and provides easy tools to help families. Families with these important tools are more likely to meet their own needs, causing a positive ripple effect, allowing them to better meet the needs of the children in their home. I highly encourage you to embrace Sue's techniques, which are not only simple but fun. I am thankful to have this book to share with the families we serve. **Judith Wilhoite, *It Takes an `Ohana Family Advocate*, Family Programs Hawaii**

It's not surprising that from her deep well of knowledge and experience, Sue Badeau would find yet another way to help children--and the adults who love them--understand and heal from trauma. Rather than 'just another coloring book in the current craze,' Badeau has penned a practical, 'let's work through this' resource that informs as it calms and comforts. **Cynthia Ruchti, speaker and author of *Tattered and Mended: The Art of Healing the Wounded Soul***

Trauma, especially repeated trauma, and the body's physical and emotional responses to trauma can significantly diminish a child's opportunity for a healthy, happy life. The effects of trauma can't be wished or punished away; caregivers and families need proven tools and strategies that actually work in the real world. "Building Bridges of Hope, A Coloring Book For Adults Caring for Children Who Have Experienced Trauma" provides tools and strategies that have been time-tested for three. The insightful and intimate understanding of trauma, provided by the Badeau family, gives others a path to healing and recovery. We will be forever grateful for the wisdom they have shared! **Grace Bauer, Executive Director, Justice for Families**

I believe Jesus has a special place in His heart for little children who were abused. In this delightful, healing coloring book, child advocate, Sue Badeau, provides practical tools for a child's healing journey. Both parents and children alike will enjoy this beautiful book. **Becky Harling, Author of *The 30 Day Praise Challenge For Parents***

Sue and Chelsea Badeau's coloring book is written from their vast personal and professional experience. They will be the wind beneath your workout wings. **Lynda T. Young, MRE, Med, Author, You Are Not Alone book series**

If you are under stress, distracted or distraught, then this adult coloring book by author Sue Badeau and her daughter Chelsea may be just the thing you need. The simple act of coloring can be calming, smoothing the rough edges of your day. There's something magical about combining colors artfully, that eases the soul and spirit. **Peggy Blann Phifer, author of *To See the Sun,* and *Somehow, Christmas Will Come.***

Introduction

Welcome to the "Building Bridges of Hope" coloring book for adults caring for children who have experienced trauma. Within these pages you will find whimsical, calming and inspiring artwork to color while learning about the short and long term effects of trauma on children and what you can do to make a difference. The text pages, facing each of the art pages, provide effective strategies, tips and tools for helping children as they journey from the pain, confusion and stress often associated with trauma to the hope and well-being associated with healing.

"Imagine learning and relaxing at the same time! This new book is just the tool to make that happen," says Irene Clements, Executive Director of the National Foster Parent Association.

National parent-support advocate Ginny Blade of the North American Council on Adoptable Children writes, *"Parenting children who have experienced trauma requires parents to revisit their own childhood, remember what brings them joy, and explore their own creativity. This unique coloring book teaches and encourages parents to take care of themselves as well as their children."*

The content of this book is condensed from the nationally-regarded training on trauma-informed care that author Sue Badeau has shared with thousands of participants in all 50 states. Drawing from her academic background in child development, professional experiences in the child welfare and juvenile justice systems and personal experience raising 22 children, many of whom experienced significant early life trauma, Sue offers a unique combination of clinical and research-based expertise with practical, down-to-earth approaches that busy parents can implement with minimal investment of time and money. The lessons, strategies and activities suggested in this book have been tried and tested by parents, caregivers and professionals from diverse backgrounds and all walks of life. Throughout the book, research and resources are highlighted. Information about all of the resources mentioned can be found at the end of the book.

The simple artwork has been designed to seed and inspire your own creativity. Several blank pages have been included where you can respond to the messages in the text with ideas and images of your own. Pulling together her own unique designs with artwork created by several of her siblings and nieces, artist Chelsea Badeau draws on her professional background in the communications arena and years of community service with children to create a unified collection of healing images.

We hope you will find hours of joyful and peaceful self-expression while also gaining valuable knowledge and skills. Enjoy!

"Faith is taking the first step even when you don't see the whole staircase."

Martin Luther King, Jr

Calm

Have you ever noticed that some people are able to stay calm even when crisis or chaos reigns? The dog is barking, the doorbell is ringing, two young children are fighting over a toy, toast is burning and upstairs something just crashed to the floor. Yet, this person is cool and unruffled as she responds to each of these provocations. While to some extent this may be a personality trait, it is also a learned behavior. This ability to stay calm in these and even more challenging circumstances is a critical skill on the road to healing and wellness.

When your brain is in a calm state, you are better able to cope with the normal ups and downs of daily life. Stress levels remain low, and your ability to concentrate, focus and think clearly is increased. When calm, you are better able to learn, assimilate new information, recall important previously learned material and integrate past and present experiences while also pursuing goals and dreams for the future. A calm brain contributes to better judgment and decision-making, increased enjoyment in life and improved interpersonal relationships.

Many people have difficulty remaining calm in challenging situations, but individuals who have experienced trauma also find it difficult to remain calm in situations that are only moderately or mildly stressful. And even the calmest person will "lose it" from time to time, particularly when the brain goes into a "high-alert" or triggered state. In these instances, it is critical to have a set of tools handy to help you quickly press the "re-set" button, restoring the brain to its calmest setting.

On the following pages, we will explore a variety of ways to improve your ability to stay calm and, when necessary, to restore calmness through:

- Understanding the trauma response;
- Using slow, controlled breathing;
- Engaging all five senses;
- Moving your body;
- Linking past, present and future;
- Connecting with family and friends;
- Developing a personal wellness plan; and
- Employing "quick fixes" when needed.

Coloring itself can be both a stress-prevention technique and a "quick fix." So enjoy coloring your way to calm as you learn about these strategies and tools. All of the techniques presented here are useful for adults, but can also be taught to children and teens who have experienced trauma in their lives as they embark on their own journey of healing and hope.

"God loves you very much, don't be afraid! Calm yourself; be strong—yes, strong!"
Daniel 10:19 (TNLB)

Architecture of Trauma

Our current understanding of trauma began when family members and friends of military veterans noticed that something was not "quite right" with their loved ones. Personality and behavior changes coupled with troubling dreams were frightening and difficult to explain. Terms such as "shell shock" and "battle fatigue" were coined to describe this phenomenon.

Over time, scientists studying these issues identified what we now know as *Post Traumatic Stress Disorder (PTSD)* to explain and begin to help individuals with these challenges. We recognized that in addition to military veterans, survivors of violent crime, interpersonal abuse, natural disasters and other forms of adversity also experienced the symptoms of PTSD. Research by Drs. Robert Anda and Vincent Felitti known as the *ACES Study* began to teach us about the lifelong effects that early-life adversity has not only on mental and emotional well-being, but also on physical health. When Dr. Peter Pecora and his colleagues researched the long term impact of foster care for their report, *Assessing the Effects of Foster Care: Findings from the Casey National Alumni Study* and later follow-up studies, they discovered that adults who spent their childhood in the foster care system experienced PTSD at nearly double the rate of military veterans. In response to findings related to children and trauma, the National Child Traumatic Stress Center was formed, providing information and resources about child trauma.

Although the PTSD label has been applied to children, in the past decade we have learned a great deal about the ways that children experience trauma – and unsurprisingly, although there are similarities to adult trauma, there are also important differences. Think about it this way:

Imagine a tornado has ripped through your community and two houses side by side sustained damage from the storm. You are the architect called in to assess the damages and make recommendations for repairing and restoring the two buildings. As you inspect these two properties, you discover that one has a strong, solid foundation and the damage is on the upper floors of the building. The second house has cracks and other types of damage to the foundation as well as in the upper floors. Your charge is to restore both houses. You are confident that you can return both of them to their original strength and beauty, but you also know that they will require very different approaches because the second house will need work on the foundation before any other efforts will be effective or successful.

When children experience trauma, the impact is on the foundation and the effects upon development can be significant. Applying all of the same strategies with children that we apply to adults with PTSD is like fixing the upper floors without attending to the foundation. The strategies included in this book are designed to support healing for children or adults whose trauma was experienced while they were children. The most important thing to remember is that there is ALWAYS hope. Regardless of how complex, chronic or challenging the trauma experience, there is always hope for healing and lasting relationships with caring adults who are the most important factor in that healing process.

"The wise man builds his house upon a rock." Matthew 7:24

Child Trauma: The Elephant in the Room

Not all children who experience trauma develop PTSD or any other diagnosable condition. In fact, some children, with the support of caring adults, exhibit great resilience and heal from their traumatic experiences with minimal intervention. Yet for many other children, exposure to trauma in their early years of life will overwhelm their capacity to cope and have a lasting impact on their health, physical, emotional and educational development and behavior.

To help us better understand child trauma, I find this definition useful:

Child trauma includes the child's physical and emotional responses to events that threaten their life or safety or the life and safety of someone critically important to the child.

This definition helps us understand why different children, even when exposed to very similar traumatic experiences, will respond differently. The individual child's response is the unique weaving together of their physical (including body and brain) and emotional processing of the traumatic event or events. An event that one child perceives as life-threatening may not be experienced in the same way by another child. This definition also helps us to understand why neglect, when a child might be continually lacking for food, shelter or affection can be just as traumatizing as abuse or other physical violence. Finally, the definition reminds us that when children, even infants, witness or absorb the sensory experience of being exposed to domestic violence they can be as traumatized as if they themselves were the victim.

Children may experience a single traumatizing event such as a serious car accident, the death of a parent, placement into foster care, or surviving a natural disaster. In other instances, the trauma is prolonged and more complex. This would include ongoing abuse, neglect, sexual harm, domestic or community violence in their neighborhood, bullying, separation from a parent in military service or frequent and frightening medical treatments.

Because the trauma response is unique to each particular child, it is often confused and mislabeled. When a child has experienced or been exposed to any of the types of events described above, they may exhibit behaviors and symptoms of attention deficit, learning disabilities, attachment disorders, oppositional-defiant disorder, childhood depression or other conditions. Thus, the trauma can become the "elephant in the room," taking up a great deal of space in the developing child's body, mind and spirit but never being appropriately addressed. If it is possible or likely that a child has experienced trauma, it is important to get a thorough trauma assessment before accepting or treating the child for any of the other conditions which mimic trauma. In this way you can be sure to get to the root of the issues and provide the best possible care and interventions for the child you love. A pioneer in developing effective trauma assessment tools is my friend James (Jim) Henry, founder of the Children's Trauma Assessment Center in Michigan (see resource guide for more information).

"Love will draw an elephant through a key-hole."

Samuel Richardson

Trauma Changes the Brain

Brain scientists talk about the "architecture of the brain," and as previously discussed, when a child is exposed to traumatic events in the formative years, the impact is on the foundation. Trauma changes critical connections and responses of the brain. For more detailed information on how these changes occur and what they look like, please check out the Harvard Center on the Developing Child videos, the booklet *"The Amazing Brain"* by Dr. Linda Burgess Chamberlain, and materials by Dr. Dan Siegel, all included in the resource section.

The good news is that, while the changes to the brain are both real and long-lasting, the brain is also considered "plastic," meaning that it continues to grow and change in response to new life experiences. Once again, we are reminded that *there is always hope for healing.* The activities described in the pages ahead—designed to utilize a full mind, body and spirit approach to healing from trauma—all increase opportunities for the brain to relearn how to respond to stressful life events by forming new connections and associations which increase calmness and the ability to cope with adversity. Before we can understand how to help the child heal from trauma, we must first understand how the brain responds to trauma triggers.

What is a trauma trigger? It is a new event or sensory experience which temporarily causes a person to *relive* a traumatic experience. When experiencing a trauma trigger, you are not *remembering* something but truly *reliving* it, not only in thoughts, but also in emotions and physical reactions. A trauma trigger can cause the same rapid heart rate, nauseous stomach, shallow breathing, loss of bladder control and other physical reactions that the original traumatic event induced. Many things can serve as trauma triggers, including a certain date on the calendar, a place, or an event such as a birthday party or riding in a pick-up truck. Frequently, triggers are sensory such as a scent, sound or visual image that is similar to the original traumatic experience. For example, if a child's trauma included a bloody scene, even the sight of ketchup, or the smell of blood may serve as a trauma trigger.

The human brain is both amazing and complex. It consists of many parts, all of which are interrelated, yet each part also has its own important functions. The regions known as the cortex (pre-frontal and sensory) are responsible for *thinking* and *executive functioning.* When the brain is in a calm state, these regions help us make sense of our experiences and the world around us. The limbic system manages emotions and memory, and the brain stem takes care of basic survival. Whenever we face significant danger, the thinking part of our brain temporarily shuts down and our brains go into "fight, flight or freeze" mode. When in real danger, this is important for survival. But the brain is not easily able to distinguish between a trauma trigger and a new, real danger. The trauma trigger literally "triggers" the survival response. When in this state, the first and most important step to help the child is not to appeal to reason or try to "talk it through" but rather to help the child's brain return to a calm, fully functioning state using the approaches suggested in the remainder of this book.

"Be transformed by the renewing of your mind." Romans 12:2

Blow Your Cares Away

Sit still for a moment.

Breathe in.

Breathe out.

Repeat.

Slower now.

Breathe in.

Breathe out.

The value of slow, intentional breathing as a method of relieving stress and enhancing wellness is as old as the beginning of yoga over 5,000 years ago, and as new as the science found in the book **The Body Keeps the Score: Brain, Mind and Body in the Healing of Trauma** by Dr. Bessell van der Kolk. Slow, focused breathing is the essential "reset" button for a brain that has been triggered into survival mode. Breathing restores calm and helps the child's brain re-engage.

There are many exercises that help us learn how to practice the slow deep belly breathing that is most effective for relieving stress and restoring calm. It is good to learn several breathing techniques that you and the child(ren) you care for can experiment with until intentional breathing becomes second nature.

One of my favorite breathing techniques to help children who have experienced trauma is to blow bubbles with them. Blowing bubbles is easy, fun and relaxing. It requires focused and controlled breathing, especially to get nice fat, round bubbles. Bubble mixtures are easy to make or inexpensive to buy. You can keep little bottles of bubble mix in your kitchen, office, car, purse, and even in a child's backpack. If the child is too worked up to engage in bubble blowing, you can simply begin blowing bubbles in the child's presence. The rhythm of your breathing will become contagious and soon the child is likely to calm down and join you. You will both be more relaxed, delighting in the sheer joy of watching bubbles float off into space.

Grab a bottle of bubble mix.

Ready, set – blow all your cares away!

Breathe.

"Remember to breathe. It is after all, the secret of life."

Gregory Maguire

Three Pillars of Trauma-Informed Care

Trauma healing: It all starts with breathing, and hopefully you now have a house, car and purse filled with little bottles of bubbles. But, what next? What else can we focus on in order to build the foundation of hope our children so urgently need? What concrete strategies, beyond bubble-breathing, can we use to nurture healing while also realigning behavior in ways that support learning and growth? In 2008, Dr. Howard Bath of Australia described what he termed the three "pillars" of trauma-informed care. These are:

- Safety,
- Connections and
- Emotional Management

A three-legged stool is useless and will not stand if one of the legs is broken or missing. All three legs are needed for balance and stability. The same is true for children—they need all three of these crucial pillars, which in turn, form the foundation for increased resilience and well-being.

It is not enough for parents or caregivers to attend to these pillars. Children must also experience safety, connectedness and emotional regulation at school and in other settings where they spend time. Therefore, an important role for parents and caregivers is advocacy. As we participate in parent-teacher or IEP (individual educational plan) meetings at school, or in appointments related to the child's health, mental health or social and recreational activities, it is important to keep these three pillars in mind and ensure that they are articulated clearly as plans are developed. We need to hone our own advocacy skills so we can become the effective champions that our children need. Some components of effective advocacy include:

- Identify strengths and needs.
- Gather information – learn about legal rights, treatment options, available resources.
- Become part of a peer support group to increase confidence and skills.
- Ask key questions – for example: *What are we doing to address my child's ability to feel safe in the hallways? Who is the one adult in the school my child can go to when she is anxious? Does this plan include specific activities designed to help my son regulate his emotions particularly during transitions?*
- Stay involved, spend time with the professionals and systems you hope to influence.
- Celebrate successes and never give up.

Throughout the remainder of this book, we'll provide information and specific activities for each of these three pillars: safety, connections and managing emotions.

"A cord of three strands is not quickly torn apart."

Ecclesiastes 4:12

Be a "Safety Bee"

How do we ensure safety for children who have experienced trauma? It is not enough to remove the source of the trauma and objectively assert that the child is now safe. The child must also *feel* safe. Consider the "fight, flight or freeze" survival response we discussed earlier. It does not require *actual* danger to trigger this response, but rather the *perception* of danger. For example, if you are walking down a dark street and you hear footsteps behind you, you don't feel safe. As anxiety builds, your body and brain prepare to fight, freeze or flee. It doesn't matter in that moment whether the footsteps belong to a kindly old lady or a would-be attacker. Your brain doesn't take time for analysis before preparing for survival. Similarly, a child who has experienced trauma may be objectively safe but may not *feel* safe.

Do you want to help children both to *be safe* and also to *feel and believe that they are safe?* Try these four **"Safety Bees."**

"Bee" observant. What situations create anxiety or retrigger trauma? With this information, you can work to reorder the child's daily schedule, routines and environment to minimize exposure to triggers and high-stress situations.

"Bee" prepared. Not all triggering stimuli can be eliminated. If the smell of pizza serves as a trigger, you can stop serving pizza at home, but your child is likely to be exposed to pizza at school or at the food court in a mall. Help the child plan ahead for safety. For example, *"The next time I think I might smell pizza, I plan to sing the song 'Old MacDonald Had a Farm' in my head to distract me. And if I still feel upset, I'll practice my SOS* (see below)."

"Bee" supportive. When the child is showing signs of anxiety or experiencing a trauma trigger, *don't* offer easy platitudes about safety, but *do* reassure the child that you will work together to create safety. Rather than saying, "Don't worry you are safe here," or "I promise to keep you safe," say *"I imagine this feels scary. Let's figure out what will help you to be safe right now."*

"Bee" smart. The developers of two excellent resources, *"Real Life Heroes" (Kagan)* and *"TARGET" (Ford and Russo)* describe the "SOS" safety strategy. Much like "Stop, Drop, & Roll" for fire safety, "SOS" can be taught to children, practiced through games and role plays and implemented whenever needed. Teach your child when feeling anxious to remember:

S is for SLOW DOWN your brain. Breathe. Blow bubbles or practice another slow breathing exercise so the thinking part of your brain can reset itself.

O is for OPEN YOUR EYES and ORIENT yourself to where you are right now. Clap your hands, plant your feet into the floor, look around the room. Recite, "I am here, this is now. I am not back there; it is not back then. I am safe."

S is for SEEK SUPPORT. Find one person you can talk to. Use the other tools in the safety plan we will build together in the pages ahead.

These four "safety bees" will increase your child's confidence and sense of safety in a wide range of every day life situations.

"No wonder my heart is glad, and I rejoice. My body rests in safety." Psalm 16:9

Connections: The CAPPD and TBRI Approaches

Loving, supportive, lasting relationships are essential for all human beings and particularly for developing children. We were created for relationships. The absence of connection and attachment can have dire consequences including loneliness, failure to thrive, health problems and even death. Building on the pioneering understanding of human attachment by Ainsworth and Bowlby, ground-breaking new research on loneliness deepens our understanding of the fundamental nature of relationships for health and well-being. Yet, children who have experienced trauma have also generally experienced broken or harmful relationships. Ensuring that each child has stable, "no matter what" connections infused with trust and unconditional love is the single most important factor in the healing process.

As parents or other adults caring for children who have experienced trauma, how can we help build and sustain trust-based relationships when the capacity for trust has been deeply damaged? Two leading experts in the field, Dr. Bruce Perry and Dr. Karen Purvis, have created effective models for building trust-based secure attachments and getting to know their work will give you a wealth of information and support on your parenting journey. Begin by watching the introductory video on TBRI by Purvis (see resource section). Follow this by utilizing the CAPPD approach for connecting with hurt children developed by Philadelphia's *"Multiplying Connections"* project, based on the work of Dr. Perry. Using this approach and practicing each of the elements is one way to nurture healthy and safe emotional attachments. These elements include (visit the Multiplying Connections website to learn more):

- **C = CALM** – When interacting with your child, be calm yourself and teach your child self-calming techniques (such as bubble-blowing, SOS or the five senses and mind-body techniques described in upcoming pages)
- **A = ATTUNED** – Be attuned to your child. Pay attention to facial expressions, body language and other cues. Be observant and learn the child's triggers. Teach your child how to "tune-in" to others so they can accurately read facial, physical and voice-tone cues and respond appropriately.
- **P = PRESENT** – Be present for your child. Pay attention to your own facial expression, body language and other cues. Communicate, "I am here, I see you, I hear you." Practice mindfulness activities so the child learns to be present in the "here and now."
- **P = PREDICTABLE**, yet flexible – Provide structure and routines without rigidity. Offer notice and explanation when schedules will change. Demonstrate consistency in your responses to behavioral challenges.
- **D = DO NOT ESCALATE** – If the child's behavior or affect escalates, do not follow suit. Practice and model being calm even in the face of stress or adversity. Be an anchor. Use your own self-calming strategies when needed.

"Loneliness . . . is the most terrible poverty."

Mother Teresa

16

"Sad-Mad-Bad"

Helping Children Manage Emotions

None of us like it when our emotions race out of control. Children with a trauma history may have both a heightened sensitivity to the emotions of others, and at the same time confusion or even inability to recognize and regulate their own emotions. The impact of early life trauma, combined with frequent exposure to trauma triggers often leaves children in a near-constant state of "high-alert," or "hyper-arousal." In this state, they are always on the lookout for danger, and are often less able to distinguish between such emotions as anger, fear and sadness. Thus, even the slightest change in an adult's affect, voice tone, facial expression or body language may be enough to signal, "danger, danger!" When the child's brain receives this message, he goes into the "fight, flight or freeze" mode we've already reviewed. In this state, the child is likely to exhibit behaviors such as running away, lashing out at himself or others, throwing or breaking things, or shutting down and becoming unreachable.

At the same time, our children may have honed the survival skill of "numbing out" and disassociating themselves from their own emotions. When difficult emotions surface, they can become upset and confused. A feeling of grief or sadness can lead to a feeling of anger, and in turn, angry behavior. Helping children to understand this "sad-mad-bad" sequence of feelings and behaviors is one way to help them gain mastery over their own feelings. Juli Alvarado's approach, *Emotional Regulatory Healing,* is particularly helpful (see resource guide).

One way for parents and caregivers to help children learn to recognize and respond in a healthy way to their own emotions and those expressed by others is to model a wide range of emotions ourselves. It's okay, even healthy, for your child to see you angry, sad or fearful. Talk about these feelings and ensure that they also see that you do not hurt or abandon them in those moments. In turn, they will learn to express and cope with these and other emotions they face.

Another tool is to use an "expressions chart" depicting multiple facial expressions and the words which describe the different emotions. Coupling this with conversation about how feeling sad is different than feeling, say, disappointed or fearful is helpful. Children can also benefit from having tools to use when they just can't find the right words to express themselves. Simple tools such as a "stop sign" to indicate when they need an emotional break give them a sense of control when emotions threaten to overwhelm them. Reading stories, role-playing with puppets, or playing games like charades are also useful ways to help children explore a wide range of emotions in the context of a safe and nurturing relationship. For many children, especially older youth, exploring emotions through art, music, dance, journaling or other forms of creative expression can be especially effective. The key is to work at it patiently, slowly and continuously until the child is able to receive and express emotions without becoming anxious, distressed or resorting to aggressive behaviors.

"The best and most beautiful things in the world cannot be seen or even touched. They must be felt with the heart." Helen Keller

Use All of Your Senses

Close your eyes and imagine the last time you saw an ocean, lake or river. Remember this experience through all of your senses. What did it look like? What colors did you see? Listen for the sounds of the waves lapping –or crashing –to shore. Remember the scents of salted air or lake breezes. Feel the sand between your toes. Taste the saltiness of the briny water. How did you perceive the connection between your body and this space?

We are sensory beings and we use our senses every day to experience, process, understand and interact with the world around us. We have already learned a little about the impact of trauma on developing brains and bodies, it should be no surprise to understand that trauma's first entry into our being is through our senses. We absorb the trauma experience through our senses and then make sense of it through the interaction of our mind, body and spirit. Nearly all of the resources I have provided to you in this book underscore the importance of recognizing that our senses must be fully engaged in the healing and recovery process.

In this segment of the book, we are going to consider the five senses of sight, hearing, touch (tactile), taste and smell (olfactory) one by one. I encourage you to create a small, portable safety toolkit for yourself, and with your child. Do not make your child's toolkit for him, but work together, experiment until you find the right items. Make it small enough to fit into a pocket, purse, lunch bag or backpack. The goal of the toolkit is to offset the impact of a trauma-trigger. While the trigger causes the child to re-experience the trauma, having access to a sensory toolkit can disrupt this process. Looking at, listening to, touching, tasting or sniffing the items in the toolkit allows a new experience, or a favored memory, to infuse the senses, re-setting the brain. This technique is effective with babies and people of all ages.

Before I expand on the toolkit idea, I want to take a moment to note that in reality there are many more than five senses including, for example, the senses of balance (vestibular), pain, spatial orientation (proprioception), intuition and more. For the toolkit, we will focus on the traditional five senses, but as we move into the pages on the mind-body-spirit connection be mindful of the full array of senses. See the resource guide for more.

As we begin creating these toolkits, we will look at tried and true examples of visual images, sounds, scents and more that have been studied and shown to have calming properties. But we don't end there. Each child, is unique and the item that provides a soothing moment of calm for one person may be the very item that increases anxiety and distress for another. So while we will start with common examples, we will finish with the unique items that create our child's individual calming toolkit. Once it has been created, be sure that key adults in the child's life including parents, respite caregivers, extended family, teachers and others know about it and are able to support and encourage the child to use it when needed.

"Deep calls to deep at the sound of Your waterfalls;
All Your breakers and your waves have rolled over me."
Psalms 42:7

Color My World

The first item in the toolkit is for our eyes. A visual image that brings a sense of calm, safety and peace just by looking at it. By the end of the next three pages, the goal is to have a comforting visual image that can always be on hand. This could be a small cut out photo to carry in a pocket or wallet, or a screensaver on one's phone. In addition to the pocket-size item, consider incorporating the soothing visual images into the child's environment – throughout the house, in their bedroom and at school.

Specific colors have been associated with a variety of healing properties or moods for centuries beginning with primitive early humans. More recently, the study of the "psychology of color" employs color within alternative medicine known as "color therapy." These studies aren't rigorously scientific, yet they have merit. For example, evidence about how colors influence both mood and behavior is frequently used in marketing.

Have you ever wondered why nearly every fast-food chain is decorated in the same colors – reds and yellows? Red is believed to trigger stimulation, appetite, and hunger. Yellow attracts attention while triggering feelings of happiness. On the other hand, due to the calming nature of the color blue, several cities around the globe have begun to install blue street lights in hopes of reducing crime and suicides. This table provides some of the commonly-held beliefs about the impact of certain colors on mood and affect:

Color	Related Emotional Responses
Red	Warmth, fear, anger, stimulates mind, raises blood pressure, intense emotions, causes people to react with speed and force
Yellow	Warmth, cheerfulness, happiness, increases metabolism, exhausting, draws attention to oneself, can be aggressive
Orange	Warmth, sensual, stimulating, fun, energetic, attention getting
Blue	Cool, calming, soothing, stable, eases pain, lowers pulse, non-threatening
Green	Tranquility, compassion, hopefulness and growth, nature, natural energy,
Purple	Wisdom, spirituality, bravery, regal, mysterious, sensual.
White	To some: pure, clean and fresh; to others: empty, stark, cold
Black	Powerful and confident, draws attention, can also be seen as scary and threatening
Brown	Soothing, comforting, protected yet also lonely

Try this experiment. Make three or four copies of the image on the next page. Over the next few days, color it with your child, each time using only two colors. For example, color it all blue and green one time; red and yellow another time. Mix and match and experiment until you find the color combination that makes your child say, "Ahhhhhh, this is relaxing to me."

"Colors, like features, follow the changes of the emotions." Pablo Picasso

Do You See What I See?

When I do trainings on using this five-senses approach to trauma-healing, I ask people to share what they consider to be the most calming or soothing images they enjoy looking at. While I get many and varied responses, I would say that the most common ones fall into these categories:

- Nature scenes, without water – for example, mountains, gardens, wooded paths
- Nature scenes with water – for example the ocean, waterfalls, a river or lake
- Animals in nature – ranging from elephants and giraffes, to lady-bugs, butterflies and birds
- Flowers, trees, growing things
- Domestic animals – including farm animals such as cows, pigs and horses, to family pets such as kittens and puppies
- A special place – a home, a room, a dining room table, a rocking chair, a tree-house or flat rock jutting over a stream
- Familiar people – pictures of a beloved grandmother, baby brother or other person who is close to me
- Generic people in motion – dancers, athletes, people doing beautiful or graceful things
- Super Heroes – with masks, capes and special powers

When trying to find out what visual image will work best for calming and soothing your child, these ideas all provide great samples to start. Go for walks together and keep a keen eye out for places or things that draw your child's eye. Go on scavenger hunts, follow treasure maps or do some geo-caching. Drive through neighborhoods and ask your child to point out interesting things to see. Look at books, art displays and family photo albums together, asking the child which images they like and why they like them. Keep in mind, however, that any particular item that may be soothing to nine children out of 10, may instead be a trauma trigger for others. If a child's trauma began by being lost or abandoned in a wooded area, trees and woodland animals may not provide calming comfort.

On the other hand, sometimes children who experienced trauma had to be extra creative in order to survive, and out of that survival story they may have unique images that will continue to serve them well when in need of soothing. For example, I knew a young woman who would hide under her bed whenever her father came home drunk. She found a niche of safety there, and didn't mind the piles of dust bunnies sharing the space with her. They became her friends and when she was older and we were doing trauma work together, she discovered that images of little gray dust bunnies were her #1 "go-to" images for restoring calm when she felt anxious.

The key is to make this a fun, bonding experience for you and your child while you also learn about the specific visual images that can be added to the child's safety toolkit.

"Though we travel the world over to find the beautiful, we must carry it with us or we find it not."

- Ralph Waldo Emerson

Your Turn – What Do You See?

Guided imagery, or therapeutic visualization techniques are approaches to using the imagination to create a safe space for inducing calm, quieting breathing and heart rates and opening the individual to new, healing thoughts and memories. Many of the evidence-informed mental health practices include some version of guided imagery. As we conclude our focus on developing visual tools for our toolkit, let's practice a guided imagery exercise. By the end of the exercise, hopefully you are able to imagine what specific visual image will work best for your personal safety toolkit, and you will have found one for your child as well! We will resume this guided imagery exercise several times throughout this book.

Take a deep breath and close your eyes.

Breathe slowly - in, out, in, out. Imagine you are in your favorite spot. It may be at home, on vacation or somewhere you went as a child. It may be indoors or outdoors.

Breathe slowly - in, out, in, out. You may be alone - It may be your own private, personal space, or you may be with others in a place you share.

Breathe slowly - in, out, in, out. The most important thing is that you feel completely safe and calm in this spot. Where are you?

Breathe slowly - in, out, in, out. What or who do you see when you look around? Are you inside or outside? Do you see a person, animal, tree or waterfall? What are the colors your eyes tune in to?

Breathe slowly - in, out, in, out. What do you see? This person, pet, place or colorful pattern is an important visual image for you – an image that helps you to feel safe and calm. Keep a copy of this image with you at all times so you can turn to look at it whenever you feel anxious, stressed, or when you face a potential trauma trigger. Help your child to find his or her special image, too. You can make a wallet or pocket-size copy, or save it as the screen-saver on your phone and computer. Tuck one in your child's back pack or lunchbox. Frame a copy to hang in the child's bedroom.

Breathe slowly - in, out, in, out. What do you see? Draw your special image on the next page.

"The eye is the lamp of the body; so then if your eye is clear, your whole body will be full of light."
Matthew 6:22

The Music of Life

The second item in our toolkit is for our ears. A piece of music or other recorded sound that is soothing and relaxing. By the end of these next three pages, the goal is for you to have your "stress management playlist" downloaded onto your phone or other listening device. Similarly, once you find the music or sounds that work best for your child, you will need to determine what kind of listening device is most appropriate to ensure that the sound portion of the toolkit can be accessible when needed. For older youth, this may be a phone or iPod, but you may have to get more creative for younger children. However, there are a number of listening devices created specifically for younger children on the market, so hopefully you will find just the right one for your child. Be sure to work with your child's school to make sure it will be okay for your child to access their special sounds when needed in the school setting. If your child has an IEP (Individual Educational Plan) this can be written into it.

As we said when looking for a visual image that brings about and supports calm, start with the tried and true and then if that doesn't work, branch out and get creative. With music, this means starting with those known to be soothing such as classical music, Indian drumming, Celtic music, flutes and piano. Research shows that it is the number of beats per minute (generally around 60) that has the most calming impact on the brain rather than the type of music itself.

Projects such as *Alive Inside* or *Music Mending Minds,* which primarily work with Alzheimer's patients have shown that music which taps into the person's memories is both therapeutic and restorative to the brain and spirit. In the same way that swing bands or sixties be-bop might help an elderly person, music that is remembered from her culture or family of origin might be what your child finds most soothing. No two people are likely to have the same playlist.

Music is not only valuable for creating or restoring calm. Music taps into deep reservoirs of emotion and for this reason music therapy is particularly effective for trauma survivors. Listening to music is powerful, writing your own, or learning to play an instrument exponentially magnifies that power. So develop your own playlist, work with each child to create his or her own, and then sign your child up to learn to play an instrument.

"For you have been my help, and in the shadow of your wings I sing for joy." Psalm 63:7

Peace Like a River

Music has many powerful, evocative and soothing qualities but it is not the only form of sound that has healing benefits. In addition to music, many people find that the sound of a human heartbeat as well as sounds found in nature, particularly those involving flowing water, bring a sense of peace and calm.

Whether it is raindrops falling outside your window as you drift off to sleep, the gentle slapping of water on the sides of a canoe as you paddle down a river, walking in the sand alongside the ocean or even the thunderous pounding of a waterfall, water soothes and renews. A short clip of waves rolling up onto the shore saved on your listening device is a double bonus, offering a treat for both the ears and the eyes. Is there a place in nature, with its soothing symphony, that is particularly special to you or your child? Capture an audio or video file from this spot and add it to your stress-busting playlist.

And then get even more creative. Sometimes the most calming sound of all is hearing gentle words spoken by a person we trust. If this is true for your child, make a simple recording of the trusted person saying something such as, "You are strong. You are brave. You will be alright." Who should say the words? It might be you – the parent or caregiver! Or, perhaps the child has not reached that stage of trust with you yet. Maybe they need these words of comfort and reassurance from a grandparent, former foster parent or older sibling. In addition to the simple recording for the purpose of the safety toolkit, are you able to record trusted adults or older siblings reading or telling stories for the child? A "lifebook" doesn't have to be confined to the pages of a book. How wonderful for a child to have a birth parent, relative, teacher or other significant person in their life record stories from the child's infancy and early years.

Don't give up if neither music, nature nor recorded voices seem to provide the calming effect your child needs. Continue to be observant. There is likely to be some sound, or set of sounds, that help your child feel safe and reset the brain into the thinking mode. I have heard many examples from people around the country. For one it was the sound of a vacuum cleaner, and for another, it was the family washer and dryer. One of our sons with special needs was particularly fond of the sound of Velcro opening and closing. A sound I might find annoying such as the hum of fluorescent lights might be sleep-inducing for another person. Once you find it, record it and keep it available as part of the safety toolkit. Share it with your child's teacher and other adults who spend time with your child.

The recorded music or soundtrack is great for all of those "as-needed" moments. But don't forget the joy and pleasure to be found when you can experience these sounds "live." Look for opportunities to go to concerts or get out in nature together with your child. This type of bonding experience is both preventative and restorative. Not to mention, just plain fun!

"There is something infinitely healing in the repeated refrains

of nature." – Rachel Carson

Your Turn – What Do You Hear?

Take a deep breath and close your eyes.

Breathe slowly - in, out, in, out. Imagine you are in your favorite spot – the spot where you feel totally safe and calm.

Breathe slowly – in, out, in, out. What do you hear in this place? Is it music? The voice of someone who loves you?

Breathe slowly – in, out, in, out. What do you hear? Perhaps the sounds that soothe you are from nature – raindrops on the grass, waves rolling on to the shore, the call of a bird or the purr of a kitten.

Breathe slowly – in, out, in, out. What do you hear? Your soundtrack might be man-made - the rhythmic hum of a car engine or washing machine.

Breathe slowly – in, out, in, out. What do you hear? Find that special sound. The one that helps you to slow your breathing, relax your jaw and unclench your fist. Record and save this sound so you can return to it when you need to reset your brain to calm. Help your child find his or her soothing sounds and record those as well. Keep the recording handy on a phone or other device, accessible on the spot when needed. Provide a copy to your child's teacher or other adults in your child's life.

Breathe slowly - in, out, in, out. What do you hear? Draw an image that reminds you of your soothing sound on the next page.

"I like to listen. I have learned a great deal from listening carefully."

Ernest Hemingway

Touch My Heart

The third item in the toolkit is for our sense of touch. We experience touch through our skin – the largest of all of our sensory organs, and what touches the skin often also touches the heart. On the next couple of pages, we will explore the importance of touch, types of touch that contribute to healing and well-being and ideas for adding something touchable to the five-sense safety toolkits we are creating for ourselves and our children.

There are many studies which show the critical importance of human touch not only for healthy growth and development but for survival. To learn more about these studies, explore the articles listed in the resource section. Some of the important benefits of healthy touch include:

- Improved cognitive development, including better learning and academic outcomes
- Increased attachment, bonding and ability to form and maintain healthy, lasting relationships
- Improved physical growth and development, including healthier immune systems
- Improved emotional regulation, ability to be calm, and less aggressive or violent behavior

Yet, children who have experienced trauma have often been subject to forms of touching that increased their trauma and contributed to sensory dysregulation. This would include the painful touches of abuse, the inappropriate touches of sexual abuse or exploitation and the lack of touch resulting from neglect or institutionalization. When caring for our children, we need to be aware of and sensitive to the painful trauma triggers that may be associated with touch while not withholding the good touch that they need to develop a sense of safety, trust, attachment and overall well-being. Some children will respond well to touch-supports we can provide ourselves in the home (Carol Kranowitz provides many tools for parents in her books). Others may have deeper sensory-motor or sensory-integration issues and may benefit from specialized treatment such as S.M.A.R.T. (Sensory Motor Arousal Regulation Treatment) or occupational therapy. (See resource list for more information).

The following tips will help you to build a healthy touch repertoire with your child:

- Ask permission before touching, saying *"Is it okay to hug you now?"* rather than *"Give me a hug."*
- Never force a child to engage in a touch-based activity, be sure your child knows she has the final say over her own body.
- Use small and frequent touches– a hand on the shoulder or pat on the back multiple times a day.
- Provide access to safe, gentle deep-pressure touch which can be calming and regulating. For example, weighted blankets, extra pillows, bean bags or weighted balls.

"There is a time for everything…a time to hug, and a time not to hug." Ecclesiastes 3:5

Touchy-Feely

On the last page, we focused on the importance of human touch for healing and well-being. Unfortunately, we can't put *people* into the portable safety toolkits we are creating, therefore we also have to consider the value of touchable *things* that induce, stimulate or support feelings of safety, soothing and calm.

Did you have something special to hug or hang onto as a child? What are some of the things that you, as an adult, are most likely to reach for when you need a little extra soothing? Many people suggest the following types of items made of fleece, soft knits or flannel:

- Sweaters or hoodies
- Socks or slippers
- Shawls or blankets
- Stuffed animals
- Pillows

These ideas provide a good starting point for you to observe and try out different touchable items with your child. Always be open to allowing the child to keep a special touchable item without regard to chronological age. It is okay for your eight-year old to have a special "blankie" or your 12-year-old to keep a favorite stuffed animal in his book bag.

Remember, as discussed on the previous page, some children will have sensory-motor issues and/or sensory dysregulation, and so they may need more unusual touchable items to feel safe and soothed. If you have a child that responds well to the deep pressure of a weighted blanket, perhaps she will also benefit from having access to small weighted items like bean bags or ankle or wrist weights for those times when crawling under a blanket is not possible or feasible.

Other children, particularly if they are on the autism spectrum, for example, may have strong adverse reactions to certain textures. Nubby fabrics like fleece or corduroy may be upsetting rather than soothing, but a hard, smooth texture like polished stone or ceramic tiles may be comforting. Still other children have responded well to prickly textures such as sandpaper or skin-contact with nature (tree-bark, mud, or sand for example).

Once you discover one or more textures that seem to bring soothing comfort to your child, look into ways that you can provide extra access to these textures throughout the day (and night) and across the different environments where they spend time. For example, if a child responds well to flannel, consider flannel sheets, flannel items of clothing, flannel "throw-pillows" in the living room and covering a lunch box or school notebook with squares of flannel. In addition, look for ways that you can provide a small "pocket-size" item in the preferred texture that the child can carry with him as part of the sensory safety toolkit.

"It was good for the skin to touch the earth... to sit or lie upon the ground is to be able to think more deeply and to feel more keenly." Oglala Lakota Sioux Chief Luther Standing Bear

Your Turn – What Do You Touch?

Take a deep breath and close your eyes.

Breathe slowly - in, out, in, out. Come back again to your favorite spot – the spot where you feel totally safe and calm.

Breathe slowly – in, out, in, out. What are the textures you are touching or feeling? The wind or breeze on your face? The nubby fabric of a sofa? Soft clothing against your skin? The hard floor under your feet?

Breathe slowly – in, out, in, out. What are the textures surrounding you, holding you, providing comfort?

Breathe slowly – in, out, in, out. What do you feel against your skin? Something warm or cool? New or worn?

Breathe slowly – in, out, in, out. What do you touch? Find the texture that brings you comfort. You know the one – just running your hands across it brings a smile to your face. Cut a square of this fabric or material and keep it with you, much like some people keep their lucky rabbit's foot in their pocket. For a child, this might be a piece of a favorite "blankie" or stuffed animal. Be sure to ask permission before you cut it up.

Perhaps it is not fabric at all but a shiny coin or a smooth stone from the brook by your house. Whatever it is, find something touchable that you can carry with you, and hold on to when you need to be grounded and soothed. Help your child to find a touchstone as well.

Breathe slowly – in, out, in, out. What do you touch? Draw an image of your special touchstone on the next page.

"Touch has memory."

John Keats

38

Feed Me!

As we continue to build our five-senses safety toolkit, we turn our attention to the sense of taste. Eating healthy food nourishes our bodies, but preparing and sharing food in the company of loved ones nourishes our hearts and spirits as well. Biblically, it is no accident that many of Jesus' miracles and parables are related to food and feeding the hungry, nor that James reminds us:

"If a brother or sister is without clothing and in need of daily food, and one of you says to them, 'Go in peace, be warmed and be filled,' and yet you do not give them what is necessary for their body, what use is that?"

Providing food is a sign of providing love, comfort and safety. The opening scene in the musical version of Dickens' "Oliver!" which begins with that marvelous song, "Food, Glorious Food" and ends with Oliver Twist daring to ask for more gruel is very telling. The workhouse boys long for food that will not only fill their bellies but their need for love and belonging. After the singing-fantasy ends, their bodies and their spirits are crushed with the cruel gruel.

Many children who have experienced trauma or those who come from, in the words of Karen Purvis, "hard places," are like the boys in "Oliver." They have not had pleasant or nourishing experiences with food. They may have gone without for periods of time, or certain foods may be trauma triggers for them. In addition, children who had very little, if any sense of self-efficacy or control over the chaos, abuse or other trauma-related circumstances in their young lives may have developed habits such as refusing to eat or hoarding food because it was one of the few things they could exercise control over. On top of this, some children with trauma histories have developmental delays which create eating and digestion problems, while others may have sensory issues effecting their tolerance for certain textures and tastes.

If you are caring for a child with food issues such as these, the Spoon Foundation has developed a website, www.adoptionnutrition.org, with a wealth of useful information and resources. Key things to remember are:

- Don't get into battles over food – be willing to compromise and give your child a degree of choice and control related to what and how much to eat.
- Be observant and aware of foods which may serve as trauma triggers and minimize exposure to them – this may involve providing alternative food options when eating outside of the home (including at school).
- Keep some food available and accessible at all times and be reassuring to your child that there will always be enough food.
- Be a role model of healthy eating habits.
- Allow and encourage your child to participate in menu planning, food shopping and meal preparation with a goal of relationship-building, not culinary perfection!

"He has satisfied the thirsty soul,

And the hungry soul He has filled with what is good." Psalms 107:9

Comfort Food

On the previous page, we talked about food-related issues that are common for children who have experienced trauma. Now, let's turn to the foods our children enjoy and work towards finding the right tasty options to include in their five senses safety toolkit.

There is something about the power of homemade soup – don't you agree? Chicken soup is an almost universal symbol of comfort food and nearly every culture has their own version of this or a similar warm, comforting dish that expresses being loved and cared for – whether it is Pho, Borscht, Posole, Matzo Ball, Egg Drop or Oxtail soup, grandmothers everywhere know that a steaming bowl of homemade soup can cure everything from the flu to a broken heart.

The best soups are made without a recipe. Handed down from one generation to the next. Small children sitting on stools in the kitchen, watching–and "helping"–their Nanna, Abuelita, Mamere or Tutu chop vegetables and toss in a "pinch" of salt or a "handful" of fresh peas. Teenagers coming in the door and immediately being drawn to the kitchen by the seductive smell of simmering soup become more open to sharing about their day as they sample a fragrant spoonful. Soup heals, brings people together and creates memories.

What are your comfort foods? Besides soups, frequent answers to this question include:
- Macaroni and cheese or other cheesy-pasta meals
- Black-eyed peas and corn bread
- Ice cream or chocolate

While the foods that we typically call "comfort foods" do produce neuro-transmitters that elevate mood, the real value is in the warm memories they evoke. Recent research has somewhat debunked the idea that any specific foods decrease stress or increase pleasure, but digging deeper, we learn that certain foods do bring comfort when they are associated with memories of being loved, valued, cared for or celebrated. (See articles in the resource section for more information on these studies.) Positive food memories evoke a sense of connection and belonging. Later, eating the same foods can reinforce those feelings even when not surrounded by the same people. It always comes back to relationships, doesn't it?

Through observation, conversation and trial and error, take the time to get to know what foods–or beverages–bring comfort to your child. Slowly, as the child's trust in you grows, learn the story behind the special foods, include these foods in your menu-planning, and add the recipes to your child's lifestory book. If your child doesn't have a special comfort food, work towards developing one or two special foods you can share together. Through this process you will discover what foods to include in your child's five senses safety toolkit.

"Soup is a lot like a family. Each ingredient enhances the others; each batch has its own characteristics; and it needs time to simmer to reach full flavor." Marge Kennedy

Your Turn – What Do You Taste?

Take a deep breath and close your eyes.

Breathe slowly - in, out, in, out. Let's return to that calm, safe spot. We've explored what we see, hear and touch while there – this time, let's imagine we are eating or drinking something.

Breathe slowly – in, out, in, out. What do you taste? Is it a bite of comfort food from your childhood? Mashed potatoes, macaroni and cheese, grandma's homemade chicken soup, or simple peanut butter and jelly?

Breathe slowly – in, out, in, out. What do you taste? Maybe your comfort food has a little kick to it – sizzling fajitas, tart kimchi, or garlicky lasagna.

Breathe slowly – in, out, in, out. What do you taste? Perhaps you are most refreshed when your sweet tooth is tickled by biting into a juicy piece of fruit, savoring a square of chocolate or slurping a cold, luscious ice cream cone before it melts.

Breathe slowly – in, out, in, out. What do you taste? For some, the most comforting taste is in liquid form – hot tea, strong coffee, cozy cocoa.

Breathe slowly – in, out, in, out. What do you taste? Know what your go-to comfort food is, and know what works for your child as well. Keep a small stash on hand. You don't need to over-indulge, sometimes a few small bites will do the trick. A chocolate kiss instead of an entire chocolate bar. You can freeze single-size portions of macaroni and cheese or another favorite meal to have on hand when comfort food is the essential remedy for a stressful day.

Breathe slowly - in, out, in, out. What do you taste? Draw an image of your favorite comfort food or drink on the next page.

"Eat honey, for it is good,

Yes, the honey from the comb is sweet to your taste."

Proverbs 24:13

Scents – Potent Triggers

We now come to the last of the five senses we are exploring for the purpose of creating our five-senses safety toolkit. The sense of smell. This sense is thought to be the oldest, most primitive of all of our senses. It certainly is powerful, particularly when it comes to triggering memories (both good and bad). Have you ever caught a whiff of a certain scent and suddenly been transported to another place and time? You are not just recalling an old memory but almost reliving the situation.

It happens to everyone, and has been described as the *Proust Phenomenon* after writer Marcel Proust. In his famous novel, *In Search of Lost Time,* his narrator experiences a powerful influx of childhood memories upon exposure to the scent of a snack with tea. The triggering scent can be a common and familiar one, such as peppermint candy-canes at Christmas, or it can be unique to the individual such as the scent of your grandparents' attic or your father's breath.

Our sense of smell is unique because of the way our brain processes it. Other sensory inputs, from our eyes, ears and skin, for example, have to pass through the portion of the brain known as the thalamus before they continue for processing. The sense of smell, however, goes directly into the olfactory bulb, a portion of the brain nestled next to the amygdala and the hippocampus – portions of the brain responsible for processing memory and emotions. Thus, scientists believe, the sense of smell is more directly "wired" in to the central headquarters where memories and emotions are stored. For these reasons, scents and odors can often serve as potent triggers for persons with PTSD or children who have experienced trauma.

Therefore, to help your child unpack their trauma suitcase it is important to recognize that scents may be responsible for many triggering episodes. Whenever your child behaves in a way that doesn't seem to fit the circumstances, it is important to consider that their reaction might be trauma-related. Take time to make note of what occurred within the hour and especially the last several minutes before the difficult behavior occurred. While it is easy to notice the who, what and where of the circumstances, it might be less obvious to take note of the odors that are present but this is an essential step in the process of identifying your child's triggers so together you can create a plan to reduce exposure to these triggers while also learning to manage emotions and behaviors when the triggers occur. There are often many scents co-mingled in a given space when an episode occurs, so you will have to be a bit of a detective, observing and recording over time, to tease out which scent seems to cause the most intense reactions. This exercise may seem tedious, but it is worth it as you help your child progress on the path toward healing.

"Remembrance of things past is not necessarily the remembrance of things as they were."

Marcel Proust

A Fragrant Aroma

As discussed on the previous page, scents can be powerful triggers, evoking often unwelcome memories causing our children to vividly relive a traumatic event. Learning to recognize these triggers in order to reduce exposure and plan strategies to manage exposure when it occurs is an important approach to the healing process. In addition, scents can also evoke positive memories as well as inducing feelings of calm and safety. It is, therefore, equally valuable to identify particular scents that help your child to de-stress or de-escalate and provide easy and regular access to these scents.

While scientific understanding of the benefits of aromatherapy still needs further study, there have been enough studies done to demonstrate that certain aromas and essential oils do seem to provide particular benefits. Specifically, studies have demonstrated the value of some scents for reducing anxiety, relieving pain and easing the symptoms of depression. Some of the scents used for these purposes include:

- Lavender
- Lemon
- Bergamot
- Orange
- Vanilla
- Eucalyptus
- Cinnamon

This list provides a starting point – you can experiment with these scents and see if your child responds well to any of them. Be careful and observant, as you do not want to inadvertently trigger a trauma reaction in your child. If you find your child does not respond well to a certain scent, set it aside and move on to other options. You and your child may not always respond well to the same scents, so be sure to observe your child's reactions, not simply those that you find most pleasing.

Once you have tried some of the standard scents listed above, you can also be creative as you notice situations in which your child seems most relaxed and regulated. What scent is in the air? Perhaps it will be the scent of a laundry detergent used at a time when the child felt safe, or a favorite food. Notice how your child reacts to different scents in nature, during the change of seasons, or when you visit a new environment. As trust grows between you and your child, use these moments as opportunities to help them explore the positive memories in their lives. Share some of your own examples as well. You will be helping your children to develop a storehouse of positive experiences to draw from during difficult times.

"Sometimes we should express our gratitude for the small and simple things like the scent of the rain, the taste of your favorite food, or the sound of a loved one's voice." Joseph B. Wirthlin

Your Turn – What Do You Smell?

Take a deep breath and close your eyes.

Breathe slowly - in, out, in, out. It's time to take one more visit to that special, safe, comforting place. And we've saved the best for last in this journey through our senses. On this visit, breathe deeply and notice what you smell while here.

Our sense of smell is powerful. Many trauma triggers are associated with a scent, but fortunately, well-chosen aromas can contribute to healing as well.

Breathe slowly – in, out, in, out. What do you smell? Is there a scent associated with a special person? Perfume? Lotion? Breath mints?

Breathe slowly – in, out, in, out. What do you smell? There might be a scent from nature that provides comfort and calming. Experts in aromatherapy suggest that scents such as lavender, eucalyptus, vanilla, cinnamon and sage have soothing properties.

Breathe slowly – in, out, in, out. What do you smell? Find the scent that works for you. Then experiment with how much of this scent is effective in creating or restoring calm in your life. You may wish to use aromatherapy candles, scented soaps, sprays or lotions, dryer sheets or other mechanisms to infuse your daily life with the scent that keeps you calm and balanced. Similarly, experiment with scents that work for your child. Create a pocket-sized sachet so a quick "hit" of the chosen scent is always within reach.

Breathe slowly - in, out, in, out. What do you smell? Draw an image that reminds you of your favorite scent on the next page.

"All Your garments are fragrant with myrrh and aloes and cassia;

Out of ivory palaces stringed instruments have made You glad."

Psalm 45:8

Peace

Over the past several pages, we have explored how to develop a portable safety-toolkit by creating items that engage each of the five senses in resetting the brain and restoring calm when the child feels anxious, fearful or experiences a trauma trigger. In addition to these individualized safety kits, each child also needs access to peaceful environments in which they feel safe, calm and free from external stressors. What does a peaceful space look like? While it will vary from child to child, there are common elements:

It is predictable and orderly. Children feel safer when people in their lives, especially adults, behave in predictable ways. This cuts through the chaos associated with trauma and lays a foundation for stability. This doesn't mean you have to be a perfect housekeeper, but rather that there is a sense of order in the environment. Items have their places. Clutter is minimized. Encourage the child to help define order in spaces they inhabit. "Where should we keep the blocks when you aren't using them?" or "Do you think tee-shirts and sweaters should go in the same drawer?" are questions that help the child feel a sense of control. Talk to the child in advance before making dramatic changes and invite their help when moving furniture or re-painting walls.

It engages all five senses. Walk from room to room in your house asking, "What are my children seeing, hearing, feeling, smelling or even tasting in this room? Are there any potential trauma triggers that I can remove? Is there anything that provides visual, auditory, textural or olfactory support to help my children become or remain calm? If not, what can I add?" Use these questions when you walk around other environments where your child spends a lot of time such as classrooms or a therapist's office. You cannot totally change these environments but simple suggestions that will help your child feel safe in these settings are likely to be welcomed.

It supports connection. Spaces that are overly confining, where individuals are isolated or where communication is difficult can be particularly challenging for children who have experienced trauma. Remember, connecting through relationships is one of the critical pillars of trauma-informed care. Safe and peaceful spaces invite connection and are laid out in ways that encourage social interaction and relationship-building.

It supports personal boundaries. While safe spaces invite and encourage connection, they also acknowledge and respect personal boundaries. Children do not feel that they have to constantly be touching others or making eye contact. In other words, there is balance between connecting with others and respecting the physical and emotional integrity of the individual. Children also need balance between spaces that encourage energetic body-in-motion activities and spaces for still, quiet moments of reflection and introspection.

"But the fruit of the spirit is love, joy, peace, patience, kindness, goodness, faithfulness, gentleness, self-control." Galatians 5:22

Tell Me a Story

From the time our children were small, they loved story time. We read books together and we loved re-telling stories of past events around the fireplace in the winter. These sessions often start with the question, "Do you remember the time when . . ." and end with howls of laughter, and occasional tears.

A few years ago, my husband and I decided to commit our own family story to the written word. Entitled, "**Are We There Yet: The Ultimate Road Trip Adopting and Raising 22 Kids**" our memoir is filled with many of the moments – silly and sad, endearing and gripping, challenging and victorious – that our family experienced in our first four decades. Writing this story required more than putting words to paper, but to some extent reliving the events we wrote about. This reliving was challenging, yet also remarkably healing and restorative.

For children or adults who have experienced trauma, one of the most critical elements of healing is learning how to make sense and meaning of their trauma stories. Helping children to put the pieces of a fractured past together into a meaningful whole is one of the great challenges and opportunities we have as parents or caregivers. As the National Child Traumatic Stress Network describes it, *creating a coherent "narrative" or story of what happened... enables them to master painful feelings about the event and to resolve the impact the event has on their life.* Effective trauma-informed interventions including Trauma-Informed Cognitive Behavioral Therapy (TF-CBT) and Structured Sensory Interventions for Traumatized Children, Adolescents and Parents (SITCAP) and Kagan's *Real Life Heroes* (all referenced in the resource section) make strong use of storytelling as a path to healing.

Stories that heal are not typically of the fairy-tale happy-ending variety. The healing power of stories is often realized through their very messiness, as the telling of even the most difficult stories allows us to see the places where we were still loved, where we exhibited strength, where God carried us across rocky terrain and where the seeds of hope for the future are planted and nurtured. Long before science proved the value of storytelling through research, our ancestors understood this intrinsically. Every tribe and community has its own powerful storytelling traditions and from these tales come the wisdom and hope that nurtures and guides every people as they form the bridges that successfully link the past to the future through and over the sometimes muddy waters of the present.

Take time to read and share stories with your children. Tell them stories about your own childhood. Tell them stories of their ancestors and people. Gently guide them in telling their own stories. Creating scrapbooks, lifestory books, or digital stories are great places to start. I have provided tools for each of these ideas in the resource section.

"Oh that my words were written! Oh that they were inscribed in a book!"

Job 19:23

Listening to Your Body

When children experience trauma, their minds and spirits are often disconnected from their bodies. Their minds need to be re-educated to become aware of their bodies, feel physical sensations and be attuned to what their bodies are telling them.

The ability to listen to yourself is managed by the part of the brain called the medial prefrontal cortex. This part of the brain has gone "off-line" in the words of Dr. Bessel Van Der Kolk, by the experience of trauma. The good news is; it can be retrained. Activating the medial prefrontal cortex requires the ability to be still and tune-in to yourself. The more you activate this part of the brain, the stronger and healthier it becomes. My friend, adoption expert and yoga teacher Lisa Maynard often says, *"Your body wants to tell you something, you just have to listen."*

Yoga is a great tool for this retraining, as are the simple exercises described below.

Tell your child you're going to play a game where you have to eat a chocolate kiss as slowly as possible, closing your eyes while the chocolate melts. The winner is the one who takes the *most* time. Ask the child to notice how the chocolate tastes and feels, but to be very, very quiet. (If your child has a chocolate allergy, you can also do this with a lifesaver mint candy.)

You can also ask your child the simple question– *What do you think your body is trying to tell you when you:*

- Get goosebumps?
- Feel your jaw getting tight?
- Have an upset tummy?

Or - *When you have this feeling, what does your body do to let you know? Do you feel:*

- Excited?
- Scared?
- Mad? Or Sad?

Once your child has a little practice, try a more involved body scan exercise together. Begin by talking about a situation that is stressful or scary. Then, provide these instructions:

- Close your eyes and notice where you feel tension in your body - (jaws, shoulders, neck, belly, chest, fingers, toes?)
- Gently rest your hand on the tense place and breathe in very slowly, imagining your breath flowing into and around that place, and then breathe out slowly.
- Repeat five to six times, then relax and see if that tense spot feels better.

Remind your children that they can do this anytime their bodies or minds feel tense so they can learn to listen to what their bodies are telling them.

"The mind cannot forget what the hands have learned."

Jon Zahourek

Whatever Moves You

Look for opportunities to introduce your children to a variety of bodies-in-motion activities until they find some that are affirming and comfortable for them.

For some children, slow, grace-filled movement will help them reconnect with their bodies in healing ways. Dance, yoga, gentle swimming and even horseback riding are all excellent activities for these children.

For other children, expelling trauma through vigorous, perhaps even aggressive physical activity will be more helpful. Thumping on a punching bag, whacking balls with a bat, running sprints around a track, rock climbing or engaging in other activities that are not only physical, but carry a hint of risk or danger may be just the ticket.

Observe your child when she is particularly content. What does she do with her body? And what about when she is out-of-sorts? How does her body give away her mood? These observations are necessary steps to help you figure out the best movement plan for your child.

Every child who has experienced trauma needs to have regular opportunities to fully use their body, gaining skills, strength, confidence and self-esteem, enjoying the sheer pleasure of play and laughter while also bringing healing to every one of their cells. You might not get it right on the first try. One of my children who had significant cerebral palsy and a prognosis that she would never walk didn't seem like an ideal candidate for dance lessons, so we tried a variety of other movement activities. But she kept telling us that she wanted to dance, so we decided to give it a whirl. Wouldn't you know it, it was through dance that she fully became herself and found healing from trauma and a new avenue for powerful self-expression. Another child seemed to have two left feet, clumsy, always falling down. But he really wanted to play sports. Did I dare to sign him up? It turned out that the regular rhythm and routines of the practice drills his coach implemented were exactly what this child needed to begin to regulate his own body and emotions.

Physically conquering something larger-than-life is also an amazing way to build self-esteem and increase healing for children who may feel powerless and out-of-control. Explore "BIG" physical activities such as learning to swim in the deep end, ride a horse, hike to the top of a mountain or paint a large mural. The more opportunities you provide, the more likely you are to land on one that reaps benefits for your child. Be sure to play *with* your child, don't always stay on the sidelines. You will both benefit.

"It takes a lot of courage to release the familiar and seemingly secure, to embrace the new…In movement there is life, and in change there is power." - *Alan Cohen*

Nurture the Spirit

Trauma touches all parts of our being – mind, emotions, body and spirit. And therefore, no healing is complete without fully engaging all parts of our being – mind, emotions, body and spirit. While spirituality can be deeply personal, it is often not recognized until it is shared and expressed in the fellowship of community.

Nurturing the life of the spirit has many benefits for children ranging from enhancing self-esteem and supporting a sense of belonging and connection, to providing an outlet for grief and instilling a sense of hope for the future. Helping children connect to their spiritual identity also gives them a chance to talk about their sense of purpose and to make meaning out of the chaos trauma created in their lives. Finally, spiritual development contributes to a child's capacity for resilience in the face of sometimes overwhelming life circumstances. Research confirms that spiritual growth and development supports positive healing outcomes for trauma survivors by enhancing social supports and coping skills while reducing risky and unhealthy behaviors. People involved in a community of faith experience less loneliness, while also learning new ways to decrease stress and achieve inner calm.

How do we nourish the spirit when caring for children who have experienced trauma? Here are a few suggestions:

A. Honor and respect the child's spiritual and religious heritage. Create a lifebook which include mementos from their spiritual history – programs from a ceremony, a special song or poem, or the spiritual meaning of their name.
B. Be aware of religious connections to the child's trauma, work to ensure safety when they experience triggers in a spiritual setting and don't force religious participation on children.
C. Expose children to a variety of spiritual activities including, but not limited to, religious experiences – such as reflective prayer, creative prayer stations (see resource guide) time in nature, and access to the arts.
D. Let children see your faith in action. Model healthy participation in a community of faith but don't limit your own spiritual activities to one hour per week. Demonstrate how your spiritual core is the anchor for everything you say and do.
E. Ask challenging questions and pose moral dilemmas for discussion. Give children the opportunity to challenge themselves and explore life issues at a deeper level.
F. When talking to children about their hopes and dreams for the future, include discussion about having a sense of purpose - what gives life meaning?

Fostering hope and nourishing the soul of children is as important as providing food to nourish their bodies and academic support to nourish their minds.

"Always be ready … to give an account for the hope that is in you, yet with gentleness and reverence."

I Peter 3:15

Your Turn – Move When the Spirit Says Move

Isn't it great to know that we don't have to rely solely on our minds to help us – or our children – heal from trauma! Our bodies and spirits are equal partners in the work of healing.

Make yourself comfortable as you breathe slowly, in, out, in, out. Take a few moments to watch your child(ren) move about when they feel most comfortable and at ease. Notice how they open up to you more after some good outdoor play, a brisk walk or silly dancing to oldies music. Pay attention to the times when they seem uncomfortable in their own bodies, stilted, awkward or off-kilter. Look for opportunities to encourage your children to participate in the bodies-in-motion activities they find most affirming and comforting.

Turn your thoughts to yourself. Breathe slowly. In, out, in, out. When do you feel most at home and at-ease in your own body? What physical activity engages your mind and emotions in healthy ways when you feel stressed, depressed or overwhelmed with life circumstances? *Close your eyes and picture a time when physical activity left you feeling both physically and emotionally energized and refreshed.*

Now add a spiritual component to your musings. Breathe, slowly, in, out, in, out. What are the settings and circumstances when your child seems most attuned to her spiritual side? Set up interactive prayer stations that invite God's presence in meaningful and creative ways. Use reflective prayer activities, allowing children to imagine themselves sitting, talking or walking with God. Ask questions and be open to discussion about bigger picture issues in life such as "why was I born?" *What are the elements for both you and your child that awaken the spirit?*

Close your eyes and continue to breathe slowly, in, out, in, out, as you reflect on your answers to these questions. Tune in to what you see, think and feel. Observe what your child sees, thinks and feels.

Use the space on the next page to draw illustrations of the activities that help you and your child to connect mind, body and spirit in your own unique and meaningful ways.

"Open yourself to the miracle of life going on around you. Sense your intimate part in the great scheme of it..." Kristin Zambucka

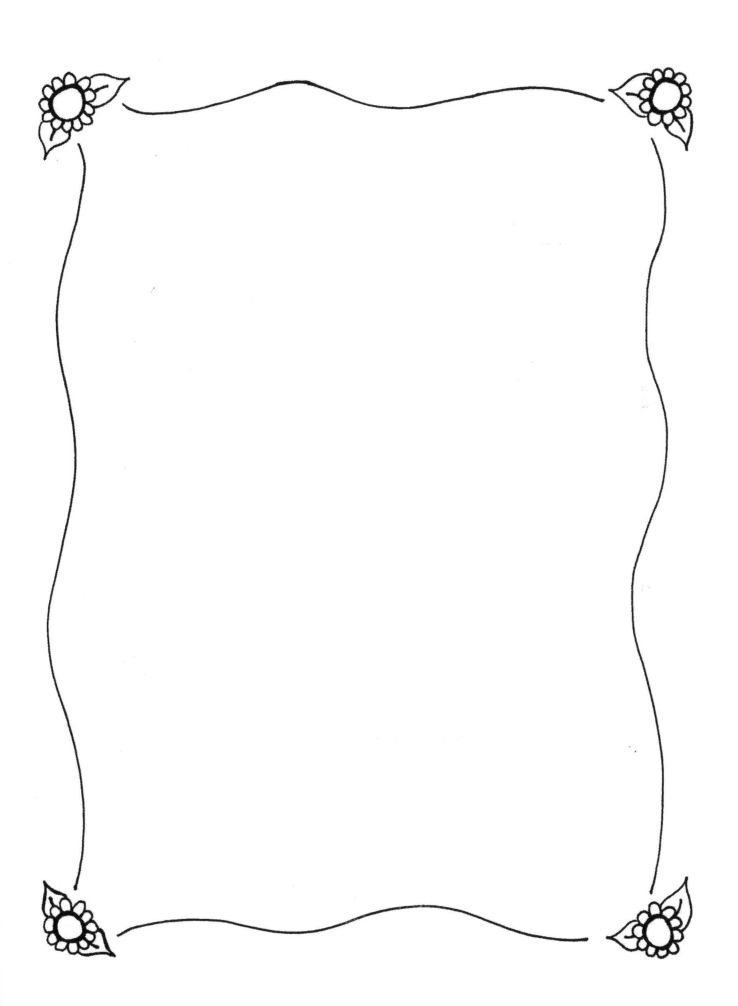

Building Bridges

Mind-body-spirit is one of two important trilogies for trauma healing. The second is past-present-future. Children who have experienced trauma often have a fragmented sense of self. The past is scary and needs to be kept locked away. The present seems overwhelming and disconnected. The future is impossible to imagine. Sandra Bloom, in her approach to trauma-healing known as the *Sanctuary Model*, encourages organizations to begin each day with a "community meeting." Among the questions often asked at this gathering are:

- What is your name?
- What is one goal you have for today? And
- What is one success you have had in the past week?

These questions are simple and yet taken together they form a brilliant template for building the bridge from the past to the future, while providing safety for the present. You don't have to be a teacher or group therapy leader to use this strategy. It works at home, too.

The first question, *"What is your name?"* is squarely in the present. Asking a child her name provides her with an opportunity to answer based on how she feels right now. Today. In the present moment. Children with a history of trauma have experienced much loss, and one of the most significant losses is their sense of self and ability to be present in the present. In the family setting, you can change this question to something like, "What nickname do you want today?" or "If you were a character in a story or movie today, who would you be?"

The second question, *"What is one goal you have for today?"* is future-oriented. For children who have lost a sense of hope, this question breaks it down to a manageable bite-sized piece. Let's just think about one day. Let's look ahead, but not so far ahead that it becomes scary.

The third question, *"What is one success you have had in the past week?"* opens the door to exploring the past. By focusing on a success, it is an affirmation and reminder that the child's entire past is not characterized by the abuse, neglect or pain of the traumatic experience but also includes positive memories and successes.

Each of these questions has value by itself, but the true brilliance of this exercise is when the questions are asked together, during the same conversation, whether at the breakfast or dinner table, bedtime or casually while watching television. Asking questions that require steps into the past, present and future within the span of a few minutes begins to help the child see herself as an integrated whole person. When you repeat this exercise every day, you are day-by-day building a true "bridge of hope." On the next few pages, we will look more closely at ways to help our children with healing and hope for the past, the present and the future.

"To everything there is a season ... A time to weep and a time to laugh;

A time to mourn and a time to dance." Ecclesiastes 3:4

The Trauma Suitcase

Several years ago, I was speaking at a conference when I received an emergency phone call to come home quickly because one of my sons was very ill and may not live. I wasn't scheduled to fly home for a few more days, so I had to rearrange my flight. I got the last seat available on the plane. I made it to Philadelphia, but my suitcase did not.

At the time, I didn't care about the suitcase, I only wanted to get to the hospital to be with my son. I am thankful for that time because he died less than a week later. Because he was a child, and because the circumstances leading up to his death were unexpected and out of our control, his death brought on not only grief, but also a trauma-response. Healing was going to take time for all of us. In fact, it is a process we are still working through.

Months later, while on a work-related trip, I got off the plane and made my way to baggage claim, expecting my suitcase to appear on the carousel. After waiting and watching everyone else retrieve their bags, it became apparent that mine was not going to show up.

Normally, this would be a slightly stressful situation. Normally, a suitcase is just a suitcase.

Not this time. This time, I lost it. Completely. I sobbed. I screamed. I stomped my feet and shook my fists. People around me probably thought I was crazy. Or that something was wrong with me. They may have whispered and pointed. Some probably backed away, while others anxiously wondered if they should intervene. Someone called security.

People around me didn't know the "back story." They didn't know that the last time I lost a suitcase, I also lost a child and that somehow, without my knowledge or permission, my brain had merged these two experiences into one and the new lost suitcase had become a trigger, causing me to relive the trauma of my son's death.

That is how it is with trauma triggers. They appear out-of-the-blue. Uninvited. Unexpected. Unwelcome.

Our children carry their past trauma around in their minds, hearts, bodies and spirits, much like I carry that suitcase around when I travel. Their trauma suitcases are filled with sensory impressions ready to leap into action at the least expected moments. I have learned to travel and even lose my suitcase from time to time without melting down in airports. Our children, too, can learn to develop the safety plans and coping mechanisms they need to unpack their trauma suitcases and live with safety and confidence. On the next page, we'll talk about unpacking the trauma suitcase.

"Sometimes a suitcase is just a suitcase... Sometimes it is more."

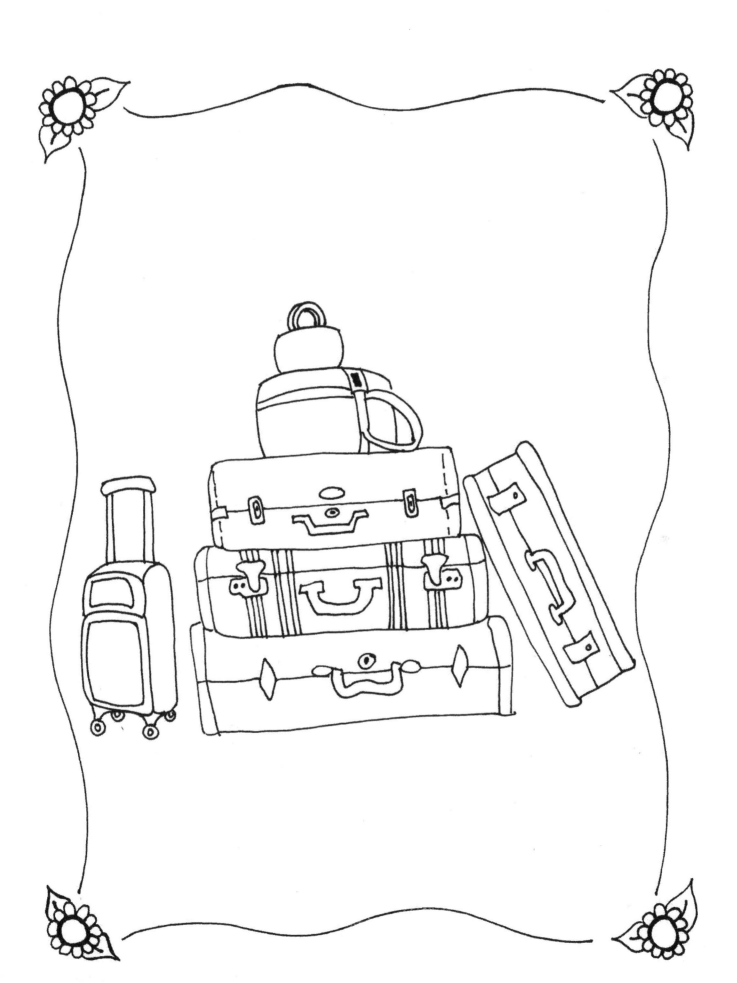

Unpacking the Trauma Suitcase

On the previous page, we learned that traveling through life after experiencing trauma is a lot like walking through a land-mine carrying a suitcase filled with painful trauma-triggers related to unhealed wounds lodged in the heart, mind, body and spirit. No wonder our children tend to avoid trips down memory lane! On this page, we will consider what helps a child unpack the suitcase and be better equipped to live without fear of the past intruding itself into the present.

Parents, teachers, social workers, foster care providers, Sunday school leaders, coaches or others who live and work with children who have experienced trauma frequently see children having meltdowns like I did in the airport - "acting out" aggressively, running away or "acting in" by crying or shutting down. In each instance, the behaviors often seem totally out-of-proportion to and out-of-sync with the situation that precipitated it. These behaviors lead to the question, "What's wrong with this kid?" and often to labels as a "bad" kid, out-of-control, attention-deficit, reactive attachment disordered, or even oppositional-defiant.

In those moments, we need to take a breath and ask ourselves – is this one of those times when the suitcase is more than a suitcase?

Joseph Foderaro of the Sanctuary Model team suggests that rather than "What's wrong with this kid?" the question to ask is "What happened to this child?" Going further, asking "What is happening in the current situation that is triggering the child to re-open an unhealed trauma-wound?" Are times when you or another adult describe a child's behavior using one of these phrases:

* Everything was fine until *out of the blue* . . . or
* *For no apparent reason* the child did . . .

These phrases provide clues that the behavior in front of you might be a trauma-response to a sensory or environmental trigger. This is the time to wonder, "Is there a back story?"

The good news is that, to help children heal, we don't need to know the answer. By simply asking the question, we can change our response to the child. Instead of backing away or "calling security" (i.e. punishment), we can respond in ways that induce calm, centered breathing (remember the bubble-blowing exercise) and help the child reset the brain. Later, we can work with the child to create a personalized safety plan using many of the techniques provided in this book. Ensure they have portable tools such as a calming image to look at, scented item, soothing audio selection, safe word or phrase and breathing exercises they can use whenever a trigger hits – whether at home, at school, on the playground or in the mall. We can also slowly, and with the support of a lifebook and trauma-informed therapist, help the child tell their own story, create their trauma narrative and then fill in the blanks with positive and pleasurable memories from their pasts. In this way, the trauma suitcase is transformed from a frightening grenade into a matter-of-fact piece of their story and identity.

"Everyone comes with baggage. Find someone who loves you enough to help you unpack."
Unknown quote, Wisdomquotesandstories.com

Finding Your Inner Peacock

Now that we've worked on the past a little bit, let's turn to the present. Children who experience trauma often feel worthless or even invisible. While at first this may appear to be a weakness, it is actually a sign of strength. The ability to "disappear" and become invisible is an important coping mechanism that protects and helps children survive unimaginably horrific life events including abuse, neglect, domestic or community violence, death or loss of parents, natural disasters and more. Yet, this very important survival skill becomes a hindrance to healing and can wreak havoc on the child's self-esteem and ability to attach, form healthy relationships and set goals for the future.

One of the best strategies for helping children to heal and live in the present moment is to assist them in finding their "inner peacock." The peacock is an interesting creature, one that has been associated in history, art and literature with beauty, nobility, integrity, holiness and even eternal life. Early Christians used the peacock as a symbol to represent the spiritual meaning of Easter and resurrection. If you closely observe the peacock, you will note that it doesn't look like much when its wings are tightly closed. It simply looks like a bird with a long, speckled tail. But the moment it spreads its wings, it can take your breath away with its beauty and strength.

Every child has a set of magnificent peacock feathers inside, waiting to be unfurled and shared with the world. Children who have experienced trauma simply hold their feathers tighter than most and need a little extra time, guidance and nurturing to discover their own inner beauty and strength. You can help a child "find their inner peacock" by

- Observing and commenting on things the child does well
- Providing opportunities for creative self-expression through art, crafts, music, dance
- Enhancing self-confidence and competence by teaching basic life skills such as doing laundry or cooking a meal
- Exposing the child to positive role models from diverse backgrounds

"Like a peacock, your beauty is multiplied when you spread your wings and show the world your stuff! Don't be afraid to be who you are - each peacock feather is flawed and imperfect, but collectively they create something of great beauty. Your flaws are what make you perfect!" Anonymous

Mindfulness

Helping children cultivate mindfulness and be fully present in the present is critically important to trauma-healing. Some of the exercises described when we discussed the mind-body-spirit connection help nurture mindfulness. It is also important to help children develop the ability to tolerate periods of silence and stillness. Don't rush to fill every moment of their time with busyness and activities. Ensure that they have some time each day that is unplugged from technology.

In addition to providing space, exercises and opportunities for children to practice being present, it is important for you to help them learn to be present by being present *with* them. When children have experienced periods of loss, grief and trauma before they even learn to write their name (as many of mine have), the greatest gift a parent or other caring adult in their life can give them is their presence.

The places in a hurting child's brain and spirit that have been harmed by traumatic life events have the best opportunity to heal when the child feels fully welcomed, accepted, heard and loved. Flooding our children's hearts, minds and spirits with our undistracted attention and presence is a primary antidote to trauma and expedites healing.

And yet . . . how many times while my children were growing up did I try to fill up the spaces with action? Doing something. Being busy.

So busy doing the "good-mom" stuff that I forgot to do the most important mom-thing.

Be there. Be present.

Stop stirring the soup. Be present.

Stop filling out permission slips. Be present.

Stop running errands. Be present.

It's the easiest and hardest part of being a parent or caregiver. The clearest and most challenging. The simplest and most complex.

How many times does God himself reassure us, His children, that He is with us? *"Be still and know"* (Psalm 46:10) *"I am with you always"* (Matthew 28:20) *"Do not fear for I am with you."* (Isaiah 41:10)

"Never be in a hurry; do everything quietly and in a calm spirit. Do not lose your inner peace for anything whatsoever, even if your whole world seems upset."

St Francis de Sales

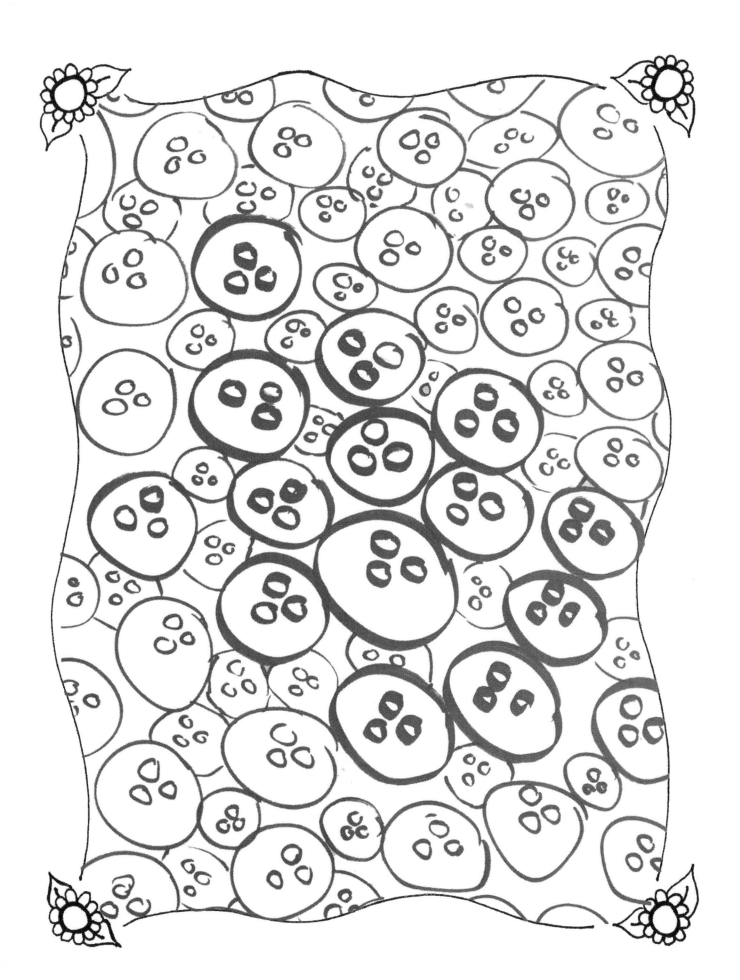

Catching Dreams

"No one ever asks kids in foster care what they want to be when they grow up," a young lady in care once announced to me. Leaning in, she whispered the rest of her thought, *"I guess it's because they don't think we'll live to grow up."*

I've never heard a foster parent, social worker or other professional in the field express their belief that children in care won't live to grow up, and yet this youngster's fear was both real and profound. It demonstrates one of the most painful ways that early life trauma scars children and teens: it robs them of the ability to hope, dream or imagine a future for themselves.

When caring for children who have experienced trauma, one of the most valuable gifts we can give them is to nurture their ability to dream. Encourage imagination and expose children to many ideas and options for their futures. In the meantime, help your child set bite-size goals. For example, "What is one thing you hope to accomplish this morning?"

Make plans together for the upcoming weekend, summer vacation, or a secret surprise for a sibling's birthday. Keep the timeframes short, gradually expanding them until the child can begin to think past next week or even next year and begin to see future possibilities unfold.

Talk to the child about your own dreams, dreams you have accomplished and those you are still pursuing. Expose them to others who set goals, dreamed dreams and succeeded, even though experiencing setbacks and challenges. Read biographies together of individuals the child admires. Engage them in activities such as music, arts, theatre or athletics where they can learn to set goals and work towards achieving them.

Each time a goal is accomplished, no matter how small, a wound from earlier trauma heals.

Each time a child musters up the courage to grab hold of a dream, bridges of healing in the brain, body and spirit are strengthened.

"Hold fast to dreams, for if dreams die, life is a broken-winged bird that cannot fly."

Langston Hughes

Stick Your Neck Out

Accomplishing goals and dreams requires sticking your neck out and taking risks.

There are two kinds of risk-taking, healthy and unhealthy (often dangerous). Children who have experienced trauma, especially teens, have a higher propensity for taking unhealthy risks, while being less equipped for taking the healthy risks that can lead to positive outcomes and hopeful opportunities for the future.

Dr. Laurence Steinberg and Dr. Kenneth Ginsburg at the University of Pennsylvania and the ACT for Youth Center at Cornell are leading experts who have researched and written extensively on this topic, and I have included materials by each in the resource section.

As parents, or other adults caring for children and teens, we can help them on a path towards a bright future by giving them the tools and skills to take healthy risks while at the same time minimizing their exposure to or access to situations where they may engage in unhealthy risk-taking behaviors.

What does healthy risk-taking look like?
- Making a new friend, or asking someone out on a date
- Entering a contest
- Speaking up in class or in the community
- Trying out for a team, play or musical group
- Running for office – team captain, class president, youth group leader
- Applying for a job, or volunteering
- Learning a risky new skill like riding a bike, swimming or driving a car

Help your child to develop the skills and confidence to engage in activities like those listed above. When possible, participate in an activity together. Work on related social-emotional skills including affect regulation, communication skills, problem-solving, conflict-resolution and decision-making. Be open to talking about your own failures as well as successes and together develop strategies for coping with setbacks and disappointments.

Look for opportunities in your child's school, church and community for youth to lead, participate in civic engagement and experience the thrills, adventures and rewards of healthy risk-taking. Research has demonstrated that this not only will help with building the resilience needed to heal from trauma, but the more a young person is engaged in healthy risk-taking, the less likely they are to engage in harmful risk-taking behaviors such as use of alcohol or drugs, unhealthy sex, or illegal activities.

"Well as giraffes say, you don't get no leaves unless you stick your neck out."

Sid Waddell

Your Turn: Dreams

"What do you want to be when you grow up?"

Grab a cool glass of lemonade or a hot cup of tea and reflect on the dreams you had as a child. What were some of your early answers to that question?

Breathe slowly - in, out, in, out. Do people consider you a dreamer? Do you look ahead to a bright future with a sense of excitement, hope and possibility?

Breathe slowly - in, out, in, out. When and how have your own dreams been nourished? What role have you played in achieving your own dreams and what roles have others – family, friends, mentors – played in supporting your dreams?

Breathe slowly - in, out, in, out. Have any of your dreams changed over time? What motivated or inspired you to change course?

Breathe slowly - in, out, in, out. Recall a time when a dream – even a small one – came true. How did that feel? Relive that feeling of accomplishment.

Breathe slowly - in, out, in, out. Think about at least one goal, or dream, that you hope to accomplish in the next five to 10 years. What will it take to turn this dream into reality? Imagine how your life will be when this dream comes true!

Breathe slowly - in, out, in, out. Close your eyes and visualize a child you care about. What dreams does this child have? What role can you play in nourishing his or her dreams?

Breathe slowly - in, out, in, out.

Use the space on the next page to draw images that remind you of your own hopes and dreams.

"Every great dream begins with a dreamer. Always remember, you have within you the strength, the patience, and the passion to reach for the stars to change the world."

Harriet Tubman

Connect

It matters not whether you win or lose, it's how you play the game." I learned this quote, attributed to Grantland Rice, from my dad. As director of high school basketball tournaments, he was known for greeting each athlete with a hearty welcome and this quote. He wanted the players to have fun, foster team spirit and leave with memories that would last a lifetime.

While not every child will be interested in sports and not every parent will commit to seemingly endless practices and games, there are definitely life lessons from team sports that apply to parenting children with trauma histories. Not every team member is on the court, field, rink or track at the same time. And yet each person who is part of the team plays a vital role.

So it is with parenting, particularly if you are caring for a child with a trauma history. It does take a village – or in this analogy a team – to meet all the needs of the child. And the child's team needs to be bigger than it looks at any one moment. Not every person who is part of the team will be present in all situations, yet each plays a vital role and the child's well being depends on this. For children, the team members in addition to parents include siblings, grandparents and other extended family, teachers, pastors, doctors, nurses, and therapists, coaches, neighbors and friends.

Who are the players on your child's team? Creating a team that strengthens and supports the child in the context of the family and community may seem like trying to put together a challenging puzzle. As you connect each person to your child and your family, the finished puzzle image emerges, appearing cohesive, strong and beautiful. Consider these questions as you pull together your child's "A" team:

- **WHO** helps keep my child **safe**?
- **WHO** will help my child grow **strong and healthy** in mind, body and spirit?
- **WHO** provides linkages for my child's past, **history and heritage**?
- **WHO** shares my **values** and will help me to pass them on to my child?
- **WHO** will give me needed **breaks**?
- **WHO** will help my child explore, **be creative** and take risks?
- **WHO** will commit to a **consistent, lasting relationship** with my child?

As we discussed when looking at the "Three Pillars of Trauma-Informed Care," relationships that are consistent and lasting are vital for developing resilience and healing from trauma. Our children's lives are richer, safer and more satisfying when we help them form meaningful connections and relationships.

"We are hard-wired for connection. There is no arguing with bio-science...

Connection, along with love and belonging, is why we are here, and it is what gives purpose and meaning to our lives." Brene Brown

Family and Home

For some, the feeling of being "home" is deeply rooted in a specific place. But for those who grew up in foster care, the military, or missionary families or those whose physical homes have been destroyed by fire, flood, tornado, hurricane or war, home is not always defined by a place.

When home is not defined by a place, what is it that makes a person utter those powerful words, "Home at last?" It might be the taste of grandma's best pie, or the smell of poppa's cigar. Maybe it is the sight of an old toolbox, or the sound of rain tapping on the roof. It may even be a dining room table set for Thanksgiving dinner's bounty. For nearly everyone, the image of "home" is loaded with memories and images that tickle the senses.

In our family, the image that conveys home most of all is a fireplace in the front entry-hall of our long-time family home. The fire always warmed not only our bodies, but our spirits, bringing us together in good times and bad. Babies were nursed here, teenagers roughhoused, grandparents drifted off to sleep. Deaths were mourned here. Many cups of coffee and cocoa were consumed, and wine glasses clinked together in toasts of good cheer. Toddlers drove their "big wheels" in circles around the couch, braids were done and undone, books read, songs sung and plans made. While standing or sitting close to the fire, the flickering light dancing and softly glimmering, stories were shared, memories were created and hearts were softened.

The fireplace image still brings about those warm feelings even though we no longer live at that big house. This is because far more than the physical spaces we tend to call home, and even beyond the sensory impressions rooted deeply in our spirits, home is always about the relationships we have there, the sense of belonging and being rooted in a family. *Connection* to meaningful, lasting relationships, as we have discussed, is a primary "pillar" of trauma-informed care, but as crucial as it is to have a village or team full of connections, it is doubly important to have a family to belong to for a lifetime. A forever family. A *"no matter what"* family.

The experience of trauma in early life frequently derails healthy attachment and can destroy a child's sense of belonging within a family. Whether the child you care for joined your family by birth, foster care, step-parenting or adoption, the trauma experience has likely shredded his or her capacity to believe that you are indeed, *the family* that will stick with her for a lifetime. This deep need to be rooted in family is no less important for older teens and young adults than it is for infants, toddlers and school-age children. This need for belonging is a fundamental human need across the lifespan. Consider the many ways that you, as an adult, still value family. It is not something we ever outgrow. On the next page, we'll consider parenting tips to help strengthen our children's sense of belonging with our families.

"God sets the lonely in families." Psalm 68:6

82

Creating Belonging

Every child needs and deserves a family for a lifetime. A family that will stand by, with and for them even in the most difficult moments. This is what I call a "no matter what" family. When the child's capacity to form, reform or sustain these lasting family attachments has been compromised by trauma, how do we help to rebuild them in the context of our daily lives?

First, it is helpful to hear how young people define having such a family. Here are a few of my favorite definitions shared with me by youth in foster care:

- I'll know I have a family when there is someone to miss me if ever I don't show up.
- Family is the people who answer when I call in the middle of the night.
- I don't need a family just for me, I hope to have children some day and I want them to have grandparents.
- I'll believe I'm part of a family when my pictures are up and I have a key to the house.

We've talked a lot in this book about using all five senses to promote healing from trauma. In a similar way, we can use all five of our senses to promote belonging. Take a tour of your home and make note –

- What does my child see on the walls, shelves, room arrangements that make him feel as though he belongs here?
- What does my child hear in this place every day that tells her she is really part of the family? Do you refer to the child as "my" son or daughter and say "our family?"
- What textures, tastes and scents does my child notice that ground him in the reality that this is truly home for all of us?

Create lifestory books with your children and ask them what elements of past memories they would like included in your home. Are there certain recipes, holiday traditions, a favorite blanket or toy? Be observant and include the child in these decisions. You don't want to hang a photo or continually prepare a recipe that inadvertently serves as a trauma trigger, but you do want to include things that help nurture security and connection.

Finally, one very important tip: Do not use forms of discipline that push the child away from you and imply shaming or isolation. For example, "go to your room," or "time-out" may have worked with other children, but for a child that has experienced trauma, these strategies simply reinforce disconnection and lack of belonging. "Time-in," as discussed by Dr. Karen Purvis and others in the resource guide is a trauma-informed alternative. Your child may not get to go play or participate in a favorite activity for a short time while on consequence, but rather than being banished from your side, the child will be with you, experiencing your presence.

" When a child loves you for a long, long time, not just to play with, but really loves you, then you become real...It doesn't happen all at once. You become. It takes a long time."

The Skin Horse to The Velveteen Rabbit by Margery Williams

Mirror, Mirror on the Wall

For children to dream big dreams and aspire to great goals, they need adults in their lives who will draw out and nurture their strengths, building upon them with encouragement and enthusiasm. Part of our role, in relationships with our children, is to be a mirror for them. A mirror they can look into while learning how to act, behave and communicate. A mirror that shows them a healthy example of how to manage emotions. And a mirror that replies, *"you are the fairest, most precious and most valued,"* when they ask that fairy-tale question, *"Mirror, mirror on the wall, who is the fairest of them all?"*

Many children who have experienced trauma are noticed more for negative behaviors than for their strengths. These children need adults willing to be intentional and creative about noticing, encouraging and rewarding positive attributes and behaviors. We need to "catch" them being good and provide meaningful and effective praise.

Research, brain science, the Bible, and even Mary Poppins all agree on the old adage I first learned from my grandmother: *"You catch more flies with honey than vinegar."* And yet some children, by their behavior, just seem to be "asking for" vinegar (i.e. punishment, anger, correction, or even shunning) more than others. Should we give false or insincere praise just to make them feel good in the moment?

No. Generic, non-specific, insincere or incomprehensible praise can actually do more harm than good. Praise is a very important tool in both the character-building and behavior management toolkits for parents and others who care for children, but to be meaningful and effective, it needs to be honest, sincere, clear, and specific.

"What a good boy you are!" is not effective, while *"Thank you for sharing those toys with Justin, I know they are your favorites, so it was very thoughtful,"* is effective. See the difference?

It is also important to notice incremental progress. For example: *"Last week when you were upset it took 15 minutes before you were able to be calm. And so you had to miss some of your play time and that was sad for you. But today, even though you got upset, you calmed down in only 5 minutes so you have more time to play. This is great progress! I can see you are working really hard on this."*

You are a relationship mirror when you demonstrate to children how they can express emotions in ways that are both honest and healthy and practice their best behaviors in a safe environment that says, *"You are valued and loved, even when you make mistakes."*

"Pleasant words are a honeycomb,

Sweet to the soul and healing to the bones."

Proverbs 16:24

86

Let Your Light Shine

As children begin to feel safe, securely attached in their relationships, and comfortable managing their emotions, there are two additional social-emotional skills we can work on that further strengthen their capacity for thriving and resilience. These are the practice of gratitude and the ability to give to others.

Many children who have experienced trauma have become accustomed to being the recipient of the services, supports and actions of others. Always being on the receiving end undermines self-esteem and reinforces a victim mindset. Often the services and supports received were neither desired nor welcome, which does not engender a spirit of gratitude. Learning and being given opportunities to both give and receive graciously is a powerful antidote to this problem.

Our children need to be exposed to expressions of gratitude that are sincere, spontaneous, frequent, and go beyond the material realm. As parents, when we feel grateful, do we verbalize it in front of our children? Do they hear us regularly giving thanks not only for material things but also for actions and generosity of spirit? Do we thank them when they show kindness? If we feel moved to utter a prayer of gratitude, do the kids hear it? Do they hear us express thanks to the grocery store clerk, school teacher, church secretary, doctor's office receptionist or anyone else who lightens our load or makes our day easier?

Gratitude is like a muscle, the more it is used, the stronger it gets. In addition to spontaneous expressions of thankfulness, it is helpful to be intentional and deliberate about setting aside time to think about what we are grateful for and express those feelings. For some, this can be part of a daily ritual, offering thanks for more than just the meal during the saying of grace, or naming something you are thankful for each night at bedtime.

Children also benefit from learning the joy of giving. As I write this, the children's song, "*This Little Light of Mine*" plays in my head. Children who have experienced trauma too often hide their lights under the bushel, fearful or incapable of letting it shine, unable to achieve their God-given potential, harness their gifts and talents or share them with the world around them. They may not know they have a light, or may not believe it will be valued. Giving to or helping others may not have been well-received and, in fact, may have led to shame or harm. So we need to help them learn to experience the joy of giving. Expose them to volunteer opportunities, let them choose their own gifts to give on birthdays or holidays rather than signing their name to a gift you selected. Engage them in conversations about where to spend your charitable dollars as a family. Model cheerful giving.

"Each one must do just as he has purposed in his heart, not grudgingly or under compulsion, for God loves a cheerful giver." II Corinthians 9:7

"Piglet noticed that even though he had a Very Small Heart, it could hold a rather large amount of Gratitude." A.A. Milne from Winnie the Pooh

Your Turn: Relationships

Do you have a favorite photo album or scrapbook? If you do, pull it off the shelf and take it to a favorite, peaceful comfortable spot. If you don't have one, find a few favorite photos or even holiday cards from friends and family members.

Sit down and breathe slowly - in, out, in, out. Open the book, photo box or cards. Savor the moment as you slowly look at the pictures or read the words.

Breathe slowly - in, out, in, out. Close your eyes and let your thoughts drift back in time. Recall a favorite memory of a spring day, a walk, a delicious meal, shared laughter.

Breathe slowly - in, out, in, out. As your favorite memories come to mind, notice who you are with. Who are the people that have been and continue to be there for you in good times, once-in-a-lifetime moments and mundane events of every day life?

Breathe slowly - in, out, in, out. Some memories are sad. Tears may flow. Let them come. Notice, again, who is with you? Who has been there to share your tears, understand your sorrows?

Breathe slowly - in, out, in, out. Think about a time you asked for help. Who did you call? If you needed to call someone for help today – who would it be? Who will you call when you need advice, a recipe, help with a child or aging parent, your car or finances?

Breathe slowly - in, out, in, out. Remember a time when you were the one reaching out, lending an ear, a shoulder, or a hand to a loved one in need. You are part of many circles of support, giving at times, receiving at other times.

Open your eyes. Draw a circle in the center of the next page and fill it with images or names of people that are part of your inner circle, your most meaningful connections. Around the outside of this circle, add the images and names of people that may come and go, touching your life for a short time, or a particular purpose.

Repeat this exercise from time to time, reflecting on those who are constant as well as the changing nature of relationships. Savor and value the consistent and lasting relationships in your life. Help your child to create their own circle of connections and post it where it will be a visible sign of being loved, supported and cared for over time.

"People come into your life for a reason, a season or a lifetime."

Author Unknown

Put Your Own Oxygen Mask on First

So far in this book, we have focused on strategies for helping our children to feel safe, connected and calm. On the next few pages, let's focus on developing our own self-care plans as parents and caregivers. When flight attendants on airplanes provide safety instructions, they always include the reminder to "put your own oxygen mask on first" when traveling with a child or anyone who might need your help.

What a wealth of wisdom in those few words. Put your own oxygen mask on first. You can't be there to care for others if you can't even breathe yourself. Simple. Profound. Not always easy.

Caregivers always want to reach out and help others first. It's in our blood. Taking time for "self-care" seems indulgent, unnecessary, or simply impossible, until the day we find we cannot breathe. This moment is sometimes referred to as "secondary traumatic stress." As we daily see and hear the grief, loss, trauma and pain of our children, we can become overwhelmed, numbed out and drained.

Taking time for "self-care" is not indulgent, it is essential. How, then do we make it a priority? We have to learn to create a self-care plan that includes strategies to *prevent* becoming overwhelmed as well as strategies to help us *cope* when we do become overwhelmed. I call these strategies "stress-busters."

It is important to have stress-busters that you can use on a regular basis. Some can be as often as daily, while others will be weekly or less frequent. We'll look at some ideas for each of these types of stress-busters on the next few pages.

In addition to frequency, it is also important to find strategies that engage us across multiple life domains and, just as we said for children, use all of our senses. So we'll think about stress-busting activities that are physical, emotional, intellectual, spiritual and social.

All of these ideas are part of a healthy personal wellness strategy, and yet even these steps are not enough for those living day-after-day deep in the trenches with children who have experienced trauma. We need to know when and how to reach out for help and support. Parents, caregivers, helpers, advocates – on the homefront, in the workplace and in the community– we must all have structures and supports in place to ensure that we can process, learn from, vent about, debrief and integrate the traumatic experiences that we are immersed in every day with the ebbs and flows of daily life.

Sometimes, we all need a little help putting that oxygen mask on and just taking a deep breath. Today, promise yourself a moment to breathe.

"Self-compassion is simply giving the same kindness to ourselves that we would give to others."
– Christopher Germer

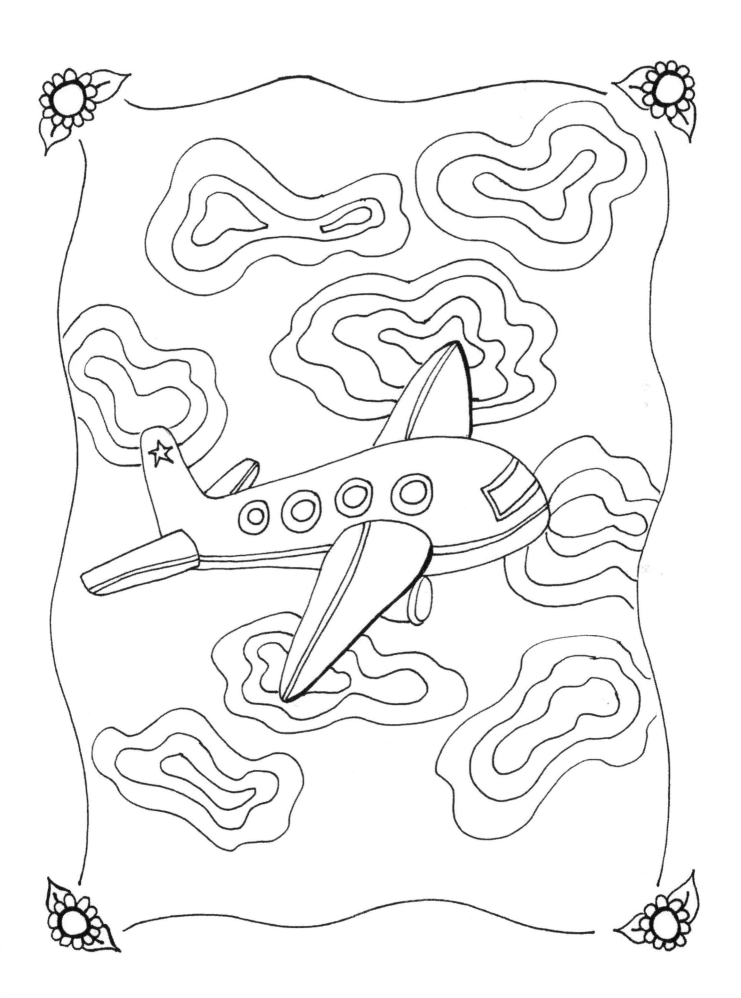

One Day at a Time

What are a few things you can do *every day* to renew and refresh your own mind, body and spirit? For me, this list includes such things as my morning devotional and prayer time, listening to music that re-charges my soul at the end of the day, doing a crossword puzzle, indulging in at least a tiny bite of chocolate and taking a walk. What are your daily "stress-busters"?

Make a list of daily activities that help you prevent stress overload, burnout and secondary trauma. Be sure to consider:

- Activities that engage each of your five senses: sight, sound, scent, taste, touch
- Activities that invigorate and stimulate your mind
- Activities that nourish and move your body
- Activities that refresh your spirit
- Activities that provide quiet time alone
- Activities that nourish relationships and time with others

Once you have made your list, copy it, post it and share it with your spouse or close friend (accountability buddy). Put it on the refrigerator, your bedroom mirror, and in the notes section of your smart phone. You won't do these things unless you remind yourself on a regular basis. You are least likely to remember your self-care strategies when you need them most. It does no good to have tools in your toolkit if the toolkit itself is out-of-sight and out-of-mind.

Think about and plan for the ways you will make the time and other necessary arrangements to implement your self-care plan. Spread your activities throughout the day and into the evening. There is nothing like a nighttime walk under the stars to restore a sense of calm after a challenging day. When we had 19 children living at home, three with chronic medical conditions, my husband found that it was worth it to get up at 4:30 each morning so he could have 30 minutes to himself before starting the daily caregiving routines. We also required even the oldest teenagers to retire to their own bedrooms by 10 at night so that mom and dad could have an hour of uninterrupted quiet time before our bedtime. When you make self-care a priority, you are not only better equipped to meet the needs of your children, you are also setting a good example for them as they learn to take responsibility for their own health and wellness.

"Yours is the day, yours also is the night; You have prepared the light and the sun."

Psalm 74:16

We Gather Together

While the daily moments for self-care described on the last page are invaluable, sometimes they are insufficient to hold the stresses of caring for our children at bay. Sometimes we need a bigger break. Something to do every week or month, something to look forward to. A weekly date with my husband, a Sunday afternoon nap after church, book club, lunch with a friend, or cuddle time with a baby grandchild all work for me – what about you – what are things you can do *every week or month* for your own well-being?

I've noticed that many daily self-care activities are solitary. They only take a few moments of time, sandwiched in between our other tasks and responsibilities. A few minutes to read, pray, exercise, sip tea, listen to music or even color in this coloring book – these things take very little time, energy or engagement with others and yet still provide a great benefit.

As we consider the less-frequent activities in our self-care toolkit, those we can do weekly or monthly, they are more often likely to include others – family members, friends, fellow sojourners on this path of bringing healing and wholeness to traumatized children. Just as meaningful connections are one of the pillars of trauma informed care for children, so, too, are relationships vital to the health and well-being of parents and caregivers.

Take time for your spouse, life partner, best friend, sister, brother. Go dancing or shopping or fishing together. Vent a little when you must, but don't forget to laugh, too, as laughter is a healthy and effective stress-management tool.

While nurturing existing relationships is terribly important, not all of our friends and family will truly understand the unique challenges or special rewards we experience as parents of children with trauma histories. Therefore, we need to cultivate new relationships, relationships with other parents walking the same path. Join a support group in your community and if you can't find one, start one. I have included tools for support group leaders in the resource pages of this book. Peer support groups provide much more than friendship or mutual griping societies. They also provide opportunities for learning and practicing new skills or banding together to advocate for our children in the communities and systems around us.

My father's favorite hymn, any time of year, was entitled, "We Gather Together." Although generally associated with Thanksgiving, he loved it year-round as a celebration of the importance of sharing our life journey in the company of others. As humans, we are created for relationships. Don't neglect yours!

"Behold, how good and how pleasant it is for brothers and sisters to dwell together in unity!"

Psalm 133:1

Unplugged

When it comes to preventing secondary traumatic stress, neither the daily nor weekly breaks described on the previous pages are enough – sometimes it takes more to truly refresh and recharge. This is when a spa day, weekend retreat, or romantic getaway – *unplugged from technology* - come into play. I can only do these things a couple of times a year, but they are so restorative! Do you have special "big" treats on your calendar?

These bigger breaks are generally referred to as respite and there is agreement that caregivers – whether parents of children who have experienced trauma, those caring for elders with Alzheimer's or other medical or mental health conditions or others in caregiving roles – need periodic respite opportunities in order to maintain the capacity to provide quality and compassionate care. Some of the benefits of respite include:

- Reduces stress and increases patience
- Enhances coping skills
- Improves energy, immune system and physical health
- Provides needed rest and improves sleep
- Provides caregiver with opportunity to gain perspective and increases hope
- Supports and strengthens the caregiver's relationships, while decreasing social isolation, depression and other potential mental health challenges caregivers may experience

Although often challenging to arrange, building respite into your life is essential. If a formal respite care program is not available to you, perhaps you can develop a "respite buddy" relationship with one or more other families so you can swap childcare a few times a year for these vital extended breaks. This is also a meaningful ministry churches could consider taking on. It is healthier for both parents and children to build respite experiences into the regular ebb and flow of your lives rather than waiting for a crisis and making emergency arrangements to get a break. Children who have experienced trauma benefit from predictability in their lives and often struggle with change. If mom and/or dad are going to go away for one or more days, it is best if it is planned ahead and the child is able to prepare calmly for the change in routine. When respite is managed in this way, it benefits both the adults and the children.

In addition to respite, every family needs time to be together in settings and circumstances unencumbered by the usual stresses and demands of school, jobs and other responsibilities. Plan at least once or twice a year to take a break together as a family. Even a mini-vacation is worth the time and effort. Never doubt the value of play, recreation and sharing new experiences on parent-child relationships and further strengthening hope and healing.

"Each person deserves a day away in which no problems are confronted, no solutions searched for." Maya Angelou

Quick Fixes

We've looked at daily, weekly, monthly and special occasion ideas for preventing, reducing, managing and coping with the stressors of daily living and/or working with children who have experienced trauma. Before we leave this theme of self-care, it is important to consider one other critical strategy. We all need a "quick fix" from time to time.

As discussed at the beginning of this book, when our children experience a trauma-trigger, their brain may go into "fight, flight or freeze" mode, effectively shutting down the thinking parts of the brain in the cortex. Thus, the most important and immediate task is to help the child "re-set" the brain, restoring a state of calm. Slow, controlled breathing, achieved by bubble-blowing, belly-breathing or similar exercises is one useful way to accomplish this.

In those moments of crisis, our own temperature is likely to rise as well. Some of us, if we have our own trauma history, may find that the child's escalation triggers our own trauma reaction and we, too, will need to reset our brains. Others, may become frustrated, agitated, angry or desperate to diffuse the situation. Our own capacity to remain calm may be compromised.

It is for moments like these that we need to know what our go-to "quick fixes" are. Using a "quick fix" is a little like applying emotional first aid. While it doesn't address the root of the issues, sometimes when we are bleeding, what we need most is a Band-Aid. What will help you remain or regain calm even when your child is escalating or in crisis mode? Experiment with some of the ideas presented in this book, and add your own until you find the one or couple of techniques that you can employ anytime, any place, as needed. Some examples include:

- Do your own breathing exercise – or blow bubbles!
- Recite a favorite calming Bible verse, prayer or mantra
- Move your body – do 10 jumping jacks, take a quick walk up and down a flight of stairs, jog in place for a minute, practice a chair-yoga exercise
- Release energy verbally – step outside or into a bathroom and belt out a scream, a laugh or a line from a song
- Practice a quick mindfulness exercise such as popping a chocolate kiss or mint into your mouth and closing your eyes while you spend 30 seconds tuning out everything else around you
- Phone a friend
- Color, doodle or draw
- Use an item in your portable "five-senses toolkit"
- OR . . .? Come up with your own "quick fix"

"Strength does not come from controlling our emotions but from learning to control how we respond to them." Guy Winch

Your Turn: Self-Care

Make yourself a cup of tea, coffee or cocoa. Put on a favorite relaxing piece of music.

Sit in a comfortable spot, with both feet squarely on the floor.

Sip your tea, then take a deep breath and close your eyes.

Breathe slowly - in, out, in, out. Visualize your breath flowing deep down to your belly and slowly circling back up and out.

Breathe slowly - in, out, in, out. Listen to the rhythm of your breaths as they slowly sync with your heartbeat and your music.

Breathe slowly - in, out, in, out. Feel the solidness of the floor (or earth) under your feet. Send your breath all the way to your toes, then back up and gently out.

Take another sip of tea. Breathe slowly - in, out, in, out. Notice the scent and taste of the tea as it mingles with your breath, flowing out to your fingers and back, up through your lungs and out.

Breathe slowly - in, out, in, out. Softly remind yourself, "I am safe. I am strong. I am courageous. I am loved."

Breathe slowly - in, out, in, out. Put on your own oxygen mask first. What does your oxygen mask look like? What are the elements in your personal self-care plan? Draw some images on the next page that can remind you to be gentle and care for yourself so you can better care for others.

"When you recover or discover something that nourishes your soul and brings joy, care enough about yourself to make room for it in your life." Jean Shinoda Bolen

Don't Forget Your Jumper Cables!

Over the years, we've taken many road trips with our children always with a well-stocked tool-kit. One of the most frequently used items is a set of jumper cables. Often, we've used them to help other stranded motorists, but occasionally we ourselves have needed this important tool.

For example, once, we parked in a scenic pull-off. After all of the kids had tumbled out of the van, we decided to take a walk into the mountains. Carrying snacks in our backpacks, we were gone several hours before we straggled back to our van. We were eager to get back on the road so we could make it to our destination before nightfall. Therefore, we were not happy campers when our van wouldn't start. Realizing we had left the headlights on, we were annoyed with ourselves and worried about how long it would be before help would arrive.

"But Dad," one of the kids called out, *"we have jumper cables!"* He stood at the rear of the van, holding the cables aloft, looking pleased as punch. The trouble was, there were no other cars in the lot. Our well-stocked toolkit was worthless until we could *connect* with someone else. Luckily, it wasn't long before another car arrived and the driver was happy to let us use our jumper cables to connect our dead battery to his live one. We were safely on our way again.

At the beginning of this book, I promised to provide a set of tools. Tools that would be useful for bringing healing and hope to a child who has experienced trauma, including:

- Understanding the trauma response;
- Using slow, controlled breathing;
- Engaging all five senses;
- Moving your body;
- Linking past, present and future;
- Connecting with family and friends;
- Developing a personal wellness plan; and
- Employing "quick fixes" when needed.

These tools are like jumper cables. While they have value, you will also find that at times, when your own battery is "dead" all the tools in your toolbox will be worthless until you can first *connect* with someone whose battery is fully charged. At times, you will be able to use your tools to recharge the batteries of a friend or family member, and at other times you will need them to return the favor. When you have the right connections – through friends, family, faith and a peer-support network and a robust toolkit, you won't avoid every danger, delay and detour on your journey, but you will have what it takes to get safely back on the road again every time.

"Abide in Me, and I in you. As the branch cannot bear fruit of itself unless it abides in the vine, so neither can you unless you abide in me. I am the vine; you are the branches."

John 15:4-5

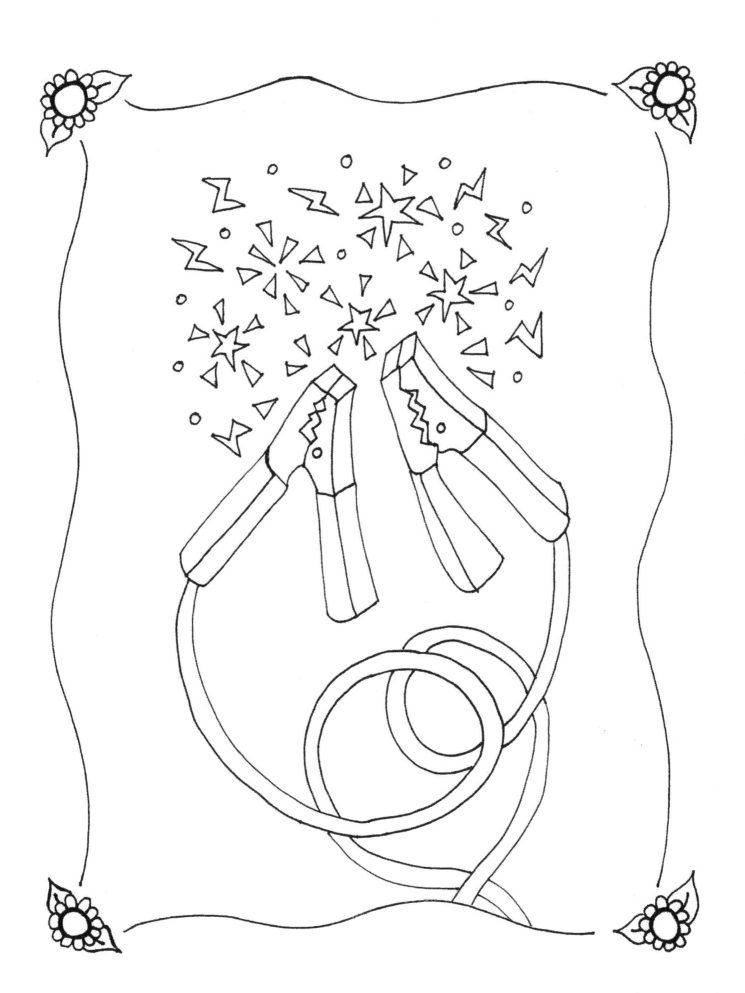

Am I Smart Enough?

My senior year in college, I couldn't decide what I was going to do upon graduation, so I took the MCAT and LSAT tests. I scored so well on both that my advisor was shocked when I decided not to apply to either law school or medical school. *"Why not?"* he asked, *"Surely you can see that you are smart enough."* Over the years, those words became a taunting refrain in my mind every time I faced a challenging situation as a parent. *"How could it be?"* I wondered, *"that I am smart enough to be a doctor or a lawyer, but not smart enough to be a mom?"* There were many, many times when I just didn't feel smart enough to conquer the challenges confronting me. At times, I felt sheepish or even ashamed when I had to reach out to others for help, resources and supports raising my own children.

And then one day, I had my "aha" moment. I was driving my adult daughter and her two-year-old child. He'd been giving her more than the usual challenges that day and they were both exhausted. She turned to me with tears in her eyes and asked, *"Do you think I'll ever be smart enough to be a good parent?"*

"Of course you're smart enough," I quickly reassured her, adding, *"but even smart people need help from time to time."* I then thought of my professor all those years ago in college and I asked my daughter, *"Do you think that I'm smart enough to be a doctor?"*

"Oh yes, mom, you definitely could be a great doctor."

"So, then, if you needed surgery today, you would trust me to wield the scalpel?"

She quietly said, *"Well, no, not really. You've never been trained as a doctor. You never went to medical school or learned all that stuff."*

Bingo. Being smart enough doesn't mean you have all the knowledge, training or tools needed to handle every situation. If I can easily acknowledge that I, while smart enough to be a doctor, cannot actually practice medicine without further education, experience, coaching and support, why can't I also acknowledge that as a parent of children exposed to trauma, I also need further education, experience, coaching and support?

There is no shame in seeking help. The jumper cables discussed on the previous page won't do us any good unless we are willing to ask the person with the live battery if we can hook ours up to theirs for a little while. We need to be willing to seek help, modeling this for our children so that they, too, will learn that it is not only okay, but healthy, to ask for help when needed.

"Be strong enough to stand alone, smart enough to know when you need help, and brave enough to ask for it." Ziad K. Abdelnour

Broken Bridges

Close your eyes for a moment and imagine this – you are driving your car as you approach a bridge you have frequently crossed before. Now imagine you have driven right up to the edge of the bridge, expecting to cross it easily and arrive in good time at your desired destination. Just as you approach the water's edge, you realize that your bridge is completely gone. Not damaged. Not fragile or weakened by a storm – but gone, it has been flooded out and washed away. Not even a remnant remains.

You stare, in disbelief, first at the destination on the other side of the water, and then at the water itself – which now looms as a huge obstacle standing between you and the other side.

What do you do?

Are you a "doom and gloom" kind of person? Do you look sadly, longingly and miserably across to your destination and say to yourself, "Well, that's it then, the damage is SO severe, I will NEVER be able to go to that destination again?

Or are you an optimist? A "glass is always more than half full" person? A person who perseveres through all obstacles and always tries hard to accomplish even the most seemingly impossible task? If so, do you look firmly at your destination and say to yourself, "I don't need a bridge! I can just drive across this water, bridge or no bridge! If I just think positive thoughts and try extra hard, I can hold on tight to the steering wheel, step down hard on the gas pedal, and varoooooom, before you know it I will be on the other side?"

Chances are you have said, "No," to both of these options. You wouldn't give up and say "never" nor would you try to drive over water without any bridge.

So what would you do? Take a few moments here and brainstorm all the possible ways you could still get to your destination. Make a list – from simple to elaborate, from "old school" to "futuristic" and everything in between. Anything goes – no idea is too basic or complex, just go wild and brainstorm! How many options can you come up with? Illustrate your ideas on the facing page.

When you turn the page, I'll process the brainstorming, gather some "lessons learned" and connect this whole exercise to helping children heal from trauma.

"Your problem is to bridge the gap which exists between where you are now and the goal you intend to reach." Earl Nightingale

Building New Bridges

Thanks for brainstorming some of the possible ways to get to your destination after a bridge is flooded out. Some ideas I've heard when I use this exercise in my workshops, include:

- Swim, build a raft or take a ferry or other boat
- Zip line or helicopter over or tunnel under
- Use GPS (or an old fashioned map) and find another route
- Build a new bridge

All of these ideas, and more, are possible. There are three keys to turning these possibilities into realities.

The first is to *believe*. Believe that it IS possible to get to your destination again, that all *hope is not lost*. There are more routes, more paths, and more options. *Believe.*

The second key is to *evaluate*. Which option will get you there fastest? Safest? Which option will cost most, or least? Which options pass the test of time? What is your priority – speed, safety, cost or sustainability? *Evaluate.*

The third key is to *act*. Don't just think about the alternate strategies for getting to your destination – take action. Make a choice and move forward. Take one step. Then another. Do something. *Act.*

As we look over all of the options, I notice that while they seem very different they *all* have three things in common.

1. Time – All of the options will take more *time* to reach the destination than if we had been able to drive over the bridge safely. Some may only take a few extra minutes, while others may take years (building a new bridge, for example).
2. Expertise – All of the options require new or different expertise, whether it is the skills needed to swim or to follow a map, or the complex set of engineering skills needed to build a new bridge.
3. Resources – Every one of the options requires resources –money, tools, materials, equipment or simply stamina, every alternate route requires resources above and beyond those needed to simply drive across the bridge.

Are you starting to see the connections between this bridge-building exercise and helping children heal from trauma? I hope so! On the next page, I will tie it all together.

"So the craftsman encourages the smelter, and he who smooths metal with the hammer encourages him who beats the anvil, saying of the soldering, "It is good"; and he fastens it with nails, so that it will not totter." Isaiah 41:7

Restoring Hope: One Bridge at a Time

On the last few pages, we have brainstormed options for getting to a destination when the usual route, a bridge, was flooded out. We learned about the three keys - *belief, evaluation, and action* – to help us get from point "A" to point "B" even in the devastating circumstance of the flooded-out bridge. Finally, we have observed the three factors that *all* of the options have in common – they all require more *time, expertise and resources,* than driving across the bridge as originally planned would have required.

Now, the time has come to tie all of this back to children who have experienced trauma.

The flooded out bridge analogy is apt because it is a reasonable representation of what happens in the child's brain when experiencing trauma. Critical linkages ("bridges") – called neuro-transmitters – are literally flooded out and washed away by the toxic levels of hormones that flood the child's brain when they repeatedly experience the "fight, flight or freeze" surges provoked by trauma or trauma triggers.

The bridge analogy also works because it underscores the inadequacy of typical responses often given to children who have experienced trauma. Many react as if the child who has experienced trauma is permanently and irrevocably damaged from the trauma. We then say this child can *never* be successful living in a permanent family, achieving in school, or thriving in the community.

Others essentially say to the child, *"Get over it. Don't let your past define you. Think positive. Try harder."* And if the child still cannot "make it" to the desired destination, we blame the child. *"She must not have been trying hard enough." "He has to learn to think more positively." "She needs to stop dwelling on her past."*

These approaches clearly don't work. The way to give children *hope* and help them to *heal* is to help them find the alternate route that works best for each child, individually.

This will mean being willing to expend time, expertise, and resources to help children heal from trauma. It also means recognizing that every child is unique so there is no "one-size-fits-all" response, yet there is *always* some response that will work. Sometimes this requires trying multiple options before finding the one that will work best for this child. In this time. And this place.

We can't know until we act. We won't act until we believe. There *is* real hope for real *healing* for every child.

"At times hope can lighten the load... other times it strengthens the bridges."

Gerald N. Lund

Resilience, Thriving, Post-Traumatic Growth and Hope

We began this book with definitions of trauma. I would like to end it with the concepts of resilience, thriving, post-traumatic growth and hope. In our yard, we had delicate pansies that grew out of the tar driveway against the brick wall of the garage; a beautiful picture of thriving and resilience in the face of unfavorable odds and adversity.

Dictionaries typically describe resilience as the ability to bounce back or recover from adversity. We know that some children seem to exhibit more of this quality than others. For example, two frightened children survive a school shooting by squeezing side-by-side under a desk. After a period of shock and grief, one emerges seemingly unscathed, strong and flourishing, while the other is gripped by a paralyzing fear and unable to move on. We call one resilient. Is it biology or parenting that makes the difference?

Nature vs. nurture: the age-old debate. In recent years, brain scientists have helped us to understand a third option. It is not nature *versus* nurture - or biology *versus* experience in some grand cosmic battle, rather it is the interplay of nature/biology *and* nurture/experience that forms, shapes and continually modifies each individual's sense of self, world-view, feelings and behaviors. Two or more children can share DNA and biology (nature). They can also share the same parenting and life experiences. Yet, they will not reflect these elements in the same way. They will require different responses from the adults in their lives in order to heal. How do we support resilience in all children? Dr. Kenneth Ginsburg, a speaker and author on the topic of resilience, describes it this way, *"Young people will be resilient when the important adults in their lives believe in them unconditionally and hold them to high expectations."*

Beyond resilience, our goal for children is that they will grow and thrive even after experiencing trauma. Scientists are now beginning to explore the concept of "post traumatic growth" which occurs when individuals not only "bounce back," but thrive after experiencing adversity. As we close out this coloring book, I'd like to leave you with a few of the key elements of both resilience and post-traumatic thriving so you can work to build or strengthen these characteristics in your child(ren). Not surprisingly, these elements begin with the three pillars we described in the beginning with a few added factors:

- Safety – both physical and psychological safety
- Connections – meaningful and lasting relationships
- Emotions – ability to manage and regulate emotions
- Self-efficacy – being valued, having ability to exercise control and make decisions
- Purpose – a sense of hope, faith, meaning and purpose in life
- An "Attitude of Gratitude" and opportunities to give and be needed.

The activities, exercises, tools and resources provided in this book will support you in your endeavor to build bridges of hope for yourself and your children.

"For I know the plans that I have for you,' declares the Lord, 'plans for welfare and not for calamity to give you a future and a hope." Jeremiah 29:11

Your Turn: Building Bridges of Hope

We've arrived at the end of the book. All that remains are the resource pages and acknowledgements. Hopefully by now, you have enjoyed many peaceful hours of coloring-induced calm while also gaining ideas, insights and tools to help you better understand and care for children who have experienced trauma.

Before you close the covers of this book, spend a few moments in a comfortable spot reflecting on what you have learned and how you can continue to make a difference. Close your eyes and breathe slowly. In, out, in, out.

It is your turn now. Your turn to build new bridges of hope for the children you care about, stone-by-stone, day-by-day. Begin with a vision of the completed bridge, and then using the tools at hand, work with patience and grace until it is completed.

Use the facing page to draw your version of a "bridge of hope." As you envision your bridge, consider these questions:

- Do I *believe* healing is possible for the child(ren) I care about?
- Have I *evaluated* the child's strengths and needs as well as my own capacity and the tools and resources available to me?
- How will I rearrange my schedule and routines to make *time* for this work of bridge-building?
- What new areas of skill and *expertise* do I need and how will I get them?
- What are the *resources* I will need and who will I turn to for help?
- Am I willing to *act* to make a difference?

Breathe slowly. In, out, in, out. You are safe. Loved. Valued. You create safety, connections and hope for children. Breathe slowly. Breathe deeply.

"Vision is the art of seeing what is invisible to others."
Jonathan Swift

Rainbows of Hope and Healing: In Poetry

These two poems, by my daughter Alysia Badeau, beautifully illustrate the difference in a young person's life when hope and healing come after trauma. Trauma creates the pain of darkness, but healing brings peace and a colorful rainbow. Dance, music, singing and writing poetry were her principle tools for trauma healing and recovery. The first poem illustrates her feelings of dark hopelessness, the second, her hopeful outlook on the future. It is my hope and prayer that each of you using this coloring book will find the tools, ideas, inspiration and calm-center from which you can be an instrument of healing, growth and hope for the child(ren) you love.

DARKNESS

Darkness –
A place where you have nobody to love
Or take care of you

Darkness sometimes gets me when I feel sad or
mad or alone

I can't breathe
I cry tears every day,

Sometimes people can't hear me
Because I'm crying
Because I'm hurt inside

I'm crying because I'm scared
People can't hear me
because I'm locked in my fear.

RAINBOW

The rainbow has
Pretty colors –
Blue, green and red and orange.
After the dark rain comes
There is a bright colorful line in the sky

The world is full of peace
The flowers are growing
The trees are flowing with beautiful
Leaves that shadow the sky
Everything is peaceful no killing, no abuse
The world is full of beauty, hope and love
Everyone is getting along without fear
Without sorrow

In my blue sky there is a rainbow in my eye
The world is alive to become peaceful
My blue sky is shining down on my eye

That rainbow shows me
feelings of beauty and color
It makes me feel good inside
It makes me feel like I am flying
in blue skylight
Rainbow colors in my eyes

Rainbows are a good part of my day
When it rains there will always be a rainbow
Looking at me
Saying colorful things to me.

"Whenever the rainbow appears in the clouds, I will see it and remember." Genesis 9:16

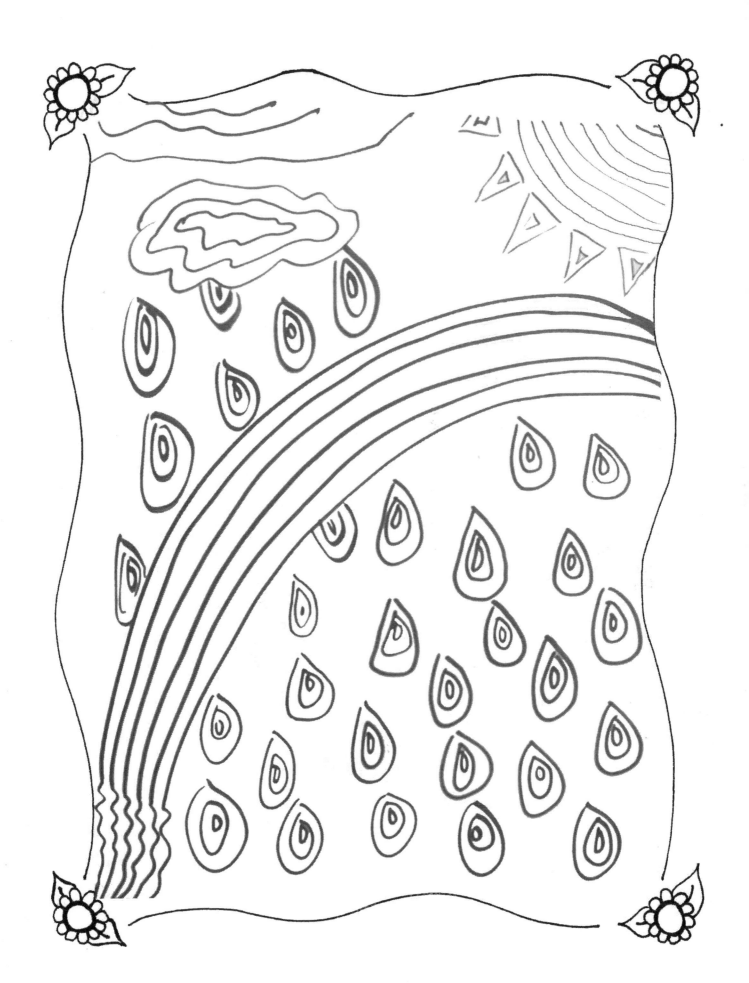

Resources Guide – Experts and Trauma-Related Websites

Information about every trauma expert, therapeutic intervention or program highlighted and research cited in the coloring book is included in this resource guide. I begin with a list of leading experts referenced in this book. Their work can be found in many of the websites, books and articles listed, and you are encouraged to dig deeper using this list as a starting point. There are many more excellent organizations and useful websites but I did not want this resource guide to be overwhelming, so I listed key sites that will then lead you to other sites and sources. Consider it a scavenger hunt! I hope you will find it to be a useful supplement to the ideas and activities provided throughout the book.

Experts Cited in this Book

Juli Alvarado	Deborah D. Gray	Lisa Maynard	Jayne Schooler
Sandra Bloom	James Henry	Bruce Perry	Dan Siegel
Linda Burgess Chamberlain	Richard Kagan	Jolene Philo	Laurence Steinberg
Kenneth Ginsburg	Carol Kranowitz	Karen Purvis	Bessel van der Kolk

Websites for Information about Childhood Trauma

ACES Study https://acestoohigh.com/category/ace-study/
Adolescent Brain, Dr. Larry Steinberg http://www.laurencesteinberg.com
Adoption Nutrition http://adoptionnutrition.org
Association for Training on Trauma and Attachment in Children: www.attach.org
Attachment Parenting International http://www.attachmentparenting.org
Center for Pediatric Traumatic Stress http://bit.ly/1Szj0gv
Child Trauma Academy http://childtrauma.org
Dr. Dan Siegel http://www.drdansiegel.com
Fostering Resilience http://www.fosteringresilience.com/about.php
Harvard Center on the Developing Child http://bit.ly/1MtV1Dw and http://bit.ly/1T4D39G
Multiplying Connections (includes CAPPD model): http://www.multiplyingconnections.org
National Center for Trauma & Loss in Children https://www.starr.org/training/tlc
NCTSN (National Child Traumatic Stress Network) www.nctsn.org
National Institute for the Clinical Application of Behavioral Medicine http://www.nicabm.com
Post Traumatic Growth Research Group https://ptgi.uncc.edu/what-is-ptg/
TCU Institute of Child Development http://child.tcu.edu
The Trauma Center at Justice Resource Institute www.traumacenter.org
Your Amazing Brain, Linda Burgess Chamberlain PhD, MPH http://bit.ly/23u7v5w

"I am not afraid of storms for I am learning how to sail my ship."
Louisa May Alcott

for Unity,
Peace, and Equality
The brain must be
Colorful

PEACE

Resources – Websites, cont.

This page provides websites related to the interventions, treatments and activities suggested throughout the book. The facing page has been left blank to provide you with space to write in additional resources you have found useful.

Treatments and Interventions Highlighted:
California Evidence-Based Clearinghouse http://www.cebc4cw.org/
Children's Trauma Assessment Center https://wmich.edu/traumacenter/directory/henry
Emotional First Aid http://www.emotionalfirstaid.co.uk
Emotional Regulatory Healing http://alvaradoconsultinggroup.com/products/
Empowered to Connect http://empoweredtoconnect.org
Music Mends Minds http://www.musicmendsminds.org/
Real Life Heroes http://www.nctsn.org/nctsn_assets/pdfs/SpeakerSeries_Kagan
Sanctuary Model http://www.sanctuaryweb.com
Sensory Smarts https://www.sensorysmarts.com/helpful_websites.html
SMART (Sensory Motor Arousal Regulation Treatment) http://www.traumacenter.org/clients/SMART.php
TARGET http://www.advancedtrauma.com/index.html
Trauma-Focused CBT - http://tfcbt.musc.edu/
Trauma-sensitive Yoga http://www.traumasensitiveyoga.com and lmaynard@sativirya.com

Activity Websites
Making Homemade Bubble Solution & Wands http://bit.ly/1VV68Xs
Creating Lifestory Books, Digital Stories & Scrapbooks http://1.usa.gov/1oXzdVh and http://www.nrcpfc.org/digital_stories/about_us.htm and http://bit.ly/23ExC6z and http://bit.ly/1S6CWbp
Coloring and Art Projects with Kids http://artprojectsforkids.org
Writing a Memoir http://jeriwb.com/writers-workout-memoir-prompts-1100/
Using Time-In, Not Time-Out, Purvis https://www.youtube.com/watch?v=T1-jOm2PyrA
Yoga and Guided Imagery with Kids http://www.cosmickids.com and http://www.guidedimageryinc.com
"Roses and Thorns" Activity http://bit.ly/1SzDqWX
Giving Effective Praise http://wb.md/1qHW8W7
Teaching Children to Pray http://www.imom.com/printable/10-ways-to-teach-your-child-to-pray/#.Vw6Fqjan5Ec
Reflective Prayer and Creative Prayer Stations http://flamecreativekids.blogspot.com/p/prayer-stations-by-children.html and http://www.rethinkingyouthministry.com/2009/02/yes-more-creative-prayer-stations.html and http://www.loyolapress.com/praying-the-ignatian-way-reflective-prayer.htm
Teaching Kids to Serve, Volunteer and Give Back http://bit.ly/1oXCbJf and http://bit.ly/1WrEylc and http://www.kathilipp.com/2014/03/can-teach-children-serve/
Creating and Facilitating Parent/Peer Support Groups and Respite Programs http://bit.ly/1YtyjvX and http://www.nacac.org/parentgroups/parentgroups.html
Self-Care for Caregivers http://bit.ly/1SzPfMK and http://bit.ly/23uEYNd

"Tell me and I forget. Teach me and I remember. Involve me and I learn." Benjamin Franklin

Resources Guide – Books

This page includes books about trauma, or books with stories that help us better understand the trauma experience of our children.

1. Badeau, Hector, and Sue Badeau. *Are We There Yet? The Ultimate Road Trip: Adopting and Raising 22 Kids!* Franklin, TN: Carpenter's Son Publishing. 2013.

2. Badeau, Sue. *Sonrise in Sweetland: Vol. 2 Set Free*. Helping Hands Press. 2015.

3. Beam, Cris. *Til the End of June: The Intimate Life of American Foster Care*. Mariner Books. 2014.

4. Bernstein, Nell. *Burning Down the House: The End of Juvenile Prison*. The New Press. 2016.

5. Bloom, Sandra. *Creating Sanctuary* (2nd ed). Abingdon, Oxon: Routledge. 2013.

6. Cacioppo, John T., and William Patrick. *Loneliness: Human Nature and the Need for Social Connection*. New York: W.W. Norton, 2009.

7. Calhoun, John A. *Hope Matters: The Untold Story of How Faith Works in America*. Laurel, MD: Bartleby, 2007.

8. Courter, Ashley. – Two Books: *Three Little Words*, and *Three More Words*. Atheneum Books for Young Readers. 2009, 2015.

9. Fisher, Nancy. *Healing Trauma Through Loving Relationships: Hope for Foster and Adoptive Families*. Create Space Independent Publishing. 2014.

10. Ginsburg, Kenneth. MD. *Building Resilience in Children & Teens*. AAP. 2014.

11. Gray, Deborah D. – Three books: *Nurturing Adoptions: Creating Resilience after Neglect and Trauma; Attaching through Love, Hugs and Play: Simple Strategies to Help Build Connections with Your Child* and *Games and Activities for Attaching with Your Child* (with Megan Clarke). London: Jessica Kingsley, 2012, 2014 and 2015.

12. Hughes, Daniel. *Attachment Focused Parenting: Effective Strategies to Care for Children* and other titles. W. W. Norton & Company. 2009.

13. Kagan, Richard. Real Life Heroes: *A Lifestory Book for Children* (3rd ed.) and *Practitioner Manual*. Abingdon, Oxon. Routledge. 2016.

14. Kranowitz, Carol. – Three books: *The Out-of-Sync Child. The Out-of-Sync Child Has Fun. The Out-of-Sync Child Grows Up*. Tarcher Perigee. 2006, 2006 and 2016.

15. McDaniel, Sharon. *On My Way Home, A Memoir of Kinship, Grace and Hope*. A Second Chance, Inc. 2014.

16. Perry, Bruce Duncan, and Maia Szalavitz. *The Boy Who Was Raised as a Dog: And Other Stories from a Child Psychiatrist's Notebook: What Traumatized Children Can Teach Us about Loss, Love, and Healing*. New York: Basic, 2006.

17. Philo, Jolene. Two books: *Does My Child Have PTSD?: What to Do When Your Child Is Hurting from the inside out*. And *The Caregiver's Notebook: An Organizational Tool and Support to Help You Care for Others*. 2014 and 2015.

"Live as if you were to die tomorrow. Learn as if you were to live forever."

Mahatma Gandhi

Resources Guide –Books, cont. and Articles Cited

This page includes a few more books and links for the articles and research cited within the coloring book.

Books, continued

18. Purvis, Karyn B., David R. Cross, and Wendy Lyons. Sunshine. *The Connected Child: Bring Hope and Healing to Your Adoptive Family*. New York: McGraw-Hill, 2007.

19. Ross, Lori. *Don't Sweat the Small Stuff: Advice from the trenches for foster and adoptive parents.* Create Space Independent Publishing Platform. 2015

20. Schooler, Jayne E., Betsy Keefer. Smalley, Timothy J. Callahan, Elizabeth A. Tracy, Debra L. Shrier, and Grace Harris. *Wounded Children, Healing Homes: How Traumatized Children Impact Adoptive and Foster Families*.

21. Siegel, Daniel J., and Tina Payne. Bryson. *The Whole-brain Child: 12 Revolutionary Strategies to Nurture Your Child's Developing Mind*. New York: Delacorte, 2011.

22. Strauss, Susan Farber. *Healing Days: A Guide for Kids Who Have Experienced Trauma*. Magination Press. 2013.

23. Ung, Loung. 3 books-series - *First They Killed My Father: A Daughter of Cambodia Remembers*. *Lucky Child*. And *Lulu in the Sky*. 2000, 2005, 2012.

24. van der Kolk, Bessel. *The body keeps the score: Brain, mind, and body in the healing of trauma*. New York: Penguin. 2014.

25. Watts, Latasha. *"I'm Not Broken Just A Little Twisted" (Scenes through the mind of a foster child)*. Cummings, Watts and Associates. 2013.

26. Wilgocki, Jennifer, Marcia Wright, Alissa Geis. *Maybe Days, A Book for Children in Foster Care*. Magination Press. 2002.

Articles and Videos – (all were retrieved 4-11-16 from the sites listed below)

1. Act for Youth Risk Taking Toolkit http://www.actforyouth.net/adolescence/toolkit/risk.cfm

2. Bath, Howard. *"The Three Pillars of Trauma-Informed Care"* https://s3-us-west-2.amazonaws.com/cxl/backup/prod/cxl/gklugiewicz/media/507188fa-30b7-8fd4-aa5f-ca6bb629a442.pdf

3. Belsky, Jay. *"Rewards are Better than Punishment: Here's Why"* http://bit.ly/1V1E5a7

4. Campaign to Change Direction. http://www.changedirection.org

5. Cherry, Kendra. *"Color Psychology: How Color Impacts Moods, Feelings and Behavior"* http://abt.cm/23EHvkA

6. Collins, Anita *"Playing an Instrument Benefits Your Brain"* (video) http://bit.ly/1SfBDMI

"How blessed is the man who finds wisdom and the man who gains understanding,

For her profit is better than the profit of silver and her gain is better than fine gold."

Proverbs 3:13-14

Resources – Articles, continued

This concludes the resource section. The facing page has been left blank to provide space for you to write in additional resources you have found helpful in your journey.

1. DiLorenzo, Paul, et al. *"Untapped Anchor: A Monograph Exploring the Role of Spirituality in the Lives of Foster Youth"* http://www.angellfoundation.org/content.php?pgID=269

2. Garrido, Sandra, et al. *"Music and Trauma: The Relationship between Music, Personality and Coping Style"* http://1.usa.gov/1SfB8lD

3. Karges, Crystal. *"Serotonin, Comfort Food and Trauma,"* http://www.eatingdisorderhope.com/blog/serotonin-comfort-foods-and-trauma

4. Konnikova, Maria. *"The Power of Touch"* http://bit.ly/1Q6WvOs

5. Kuban, Caelan. *"Structured Sensory Interventions for Traumatized Children, Adolescents and Parents: SITCAP in Action"* https://www.starr.org/sites/default/files/Structured%20Sensory%20Interventions.pdf

6. Madden, Blake. *"Music as Medicine: How Performing and Listening Treat Trauma"* http://bit.ly/1qRevs8

7. Malchiodi, Cathy. *"Visual Journaling, Self-Regulation and Stress Reduction"* http://bit.ly/1T3Y6ZY

8. Mercola, Joseph. *"Why Smells Can Trigger Strong Memories"* http://articles.mercola.com/sites/articles/archive/2015/08/06/smells-trigger-memories.aspx

9. O'Brien, Pat. *"Laughter, Attachment and Adopting Older Kids"* https://www.pactadopt.org/app/servlet/documentapp.DisplayDocument?DocID=257

10. Pecora Peter, et al. *"Improving Family Foster Care: Findings from the Northwest Foster Care Alumni Study"* http://www.casey.org/northwest-alumni-study/

11. Portraits of Professional Caregivers: Their Passion, Their Pain http://caregiversfilm.com

12. Romm, Cari, *"Why Comfort Food Comforts"* http://www.theatlantic.com/health/archive/2015/04/why-comfort-food-comforts/389613/

13. University of Maryland Medical Center, *"Aromatherapy"* http://umm.edu/health/medical/altmed/treatment/aromatherapy

14. University of Nevada, Reno, *"Releasing Stress Through the Power of Music"* http://bit.ly/1N8xLLk

15. U.S. Department of Veterans Affairs. *"Spirituality and Trauma: Professionals Working Together"* http://1.usa.gov/1qHZ3y6

16. Williams, Ray. *"8 Reasons Why we Need Human Touch Now More Than Ever"* http://bit.ly/1SzNleZ

"Be careful never to forget what you yourself have seen. Do not let these memories escape from your mind as long as you live! And be sure to pass them on to your children and grandchildren."
Deuteronomy 4:9 (TNLB)

About the Author and Artists

Sue Badeau

The author, Sue Badeau, is a nationally known speaker, writer and consultant with a heart for children and families. After receiving a degree in Early Childhood Education from Smith College, Sue worked for many years in child services and serves on several national boards including the North American Council on Adoptable Children and Justice for Families. She has worked closely with the National Child Traumatic Stress Network, the National Council for Juvenile and Family Court Judges, Casey Family Programs and the Pew Commission on Children in Foster Care. Sue and her husband, Hector, are lifetime parents of 22 children, two by birth and 20 adopted. They have also served as foster parents and kin caregivers. They have authored a book about their family's parenting journey, *Are We There Yet: The Ultimate Road Trip, Adopting and Raising 22 Kids.* Sue may be reached at sue@suebadeau.com. Sue and Hector live in Philadelphia and are active in their community, Project HOME and Summit Presbyterian Church.

Chelsea Badeau

The principle artist and designer for this book is Chelsea Badeau. Chelsea is the director of editorial operations for a national media organization. She has an extensive background in creating and teaching art, including painting murals in the Philadelphia Family Courthouse and a church in Nanyuki, Kenya, as well as leading group painting sessions with her mom, Sue Badeau, on stress management techniques for caregivers of children who have experienced trauma. Chelsea graduated from Arcadia University and is an alum of City Year (an Americorps program), the FBI Citizens Academy and Leadership Philadelphia. She remains very active in her community and church by serving on boards, running volunteer projects and teaching Sunday School. She lives with her two daughters in Philadelphia, spending many nights and weekends at sporting events with her children. Chelsea can be reached at chelsbadeau@aol.com.

Contributing Artists

Sue and Chelsea wish to offer great appreciation to the following contributors for adding to the uniqueness, diversity and richness of this book. **Alysia Badeau** contributed poetry (page 118) and the following five guest artists added images for coloring. The titles and page numbers for their artwork is listed next to their names:

Abel Badeau – House (5), Heart-Hands (35), Teddy Bear (85), Toolbox (111), Colorful Brain (121)

Angel Vargas – Headphones (29), Comfort Foods (41), Coffee Mug (43), Open Suitcase (69)

Emma Wyrocki – Waterfall (31)

Kandia Kovacs – Mermaid (21) Peacock (71), Giraffe (77)

SueAnn Badeau Vargas – Brain (9), Circles (23), Mountains (25), Hands (37), Dandelion (47), Buttons (73), Dreamcatchers (75 and 125), Squares (87), Candles (89), Hearts (95) Triangles (107), Rainbow (119), Berries (127)

"Art is the stored honey of the human soul." Theodore Dreiser

Free Stuff and Discounts!

We hope you enjoyed coloring the pages in this book while learning more about caring for children who have experienced trauma. Would you like a few bonus pages to color? We invite you to visit www.suebadeau.com and click on "Freebies" where you will find a set of **three additional unique coloring pages by Chelsea Badeau to download, print and color.**

- While you are on the website, you can learn more about inviting Sue to speak, or Sue and Chelsea to do a painting and self-care workshop for you organization.

Finally, if you use the coupon below, you are entitled to your choice of $5.00 off one book or "Buy one, Get one" when you purchase two or more print versions of Sue and Hector Badeau's memoir, *"Are We There Yet? The Ultimate Road Trip, Adopting and Raising 22 Kids."* The coupon also entitles you to $2.00 off print versions of any of Sue's other titles, including:

- *Clean Heart, Renewed Joy: A Six Week Journey Through Psalm 51*
- *No Matter What: A Glimpse into the Heart of Adoption*
- *Summer in Sweetland: Complete Series*
- *Tis the Season in Sweetland: Complete Series*
- *Christmases Past: Complete Series*

HECTOR and SUE BADEAU

Are We There Yet?
THE ULTIMATE ROAD TRIP,
ADOPTING & RAISING 22 KIDS

Money Saving Coupon
Visit www.suebadeau.com
Use Coupon Code: Color2016
Save $5 or more

"Are we There Yet? The Ultimate Road Trip Adopting and Raising 22 Kids
$5.00 Off A Single Copy
OR **Buy One, Get One Free for two or more copies** OR
$2.00 off a single print copy of any of Sue's other titles listed on www.suebadeau.com

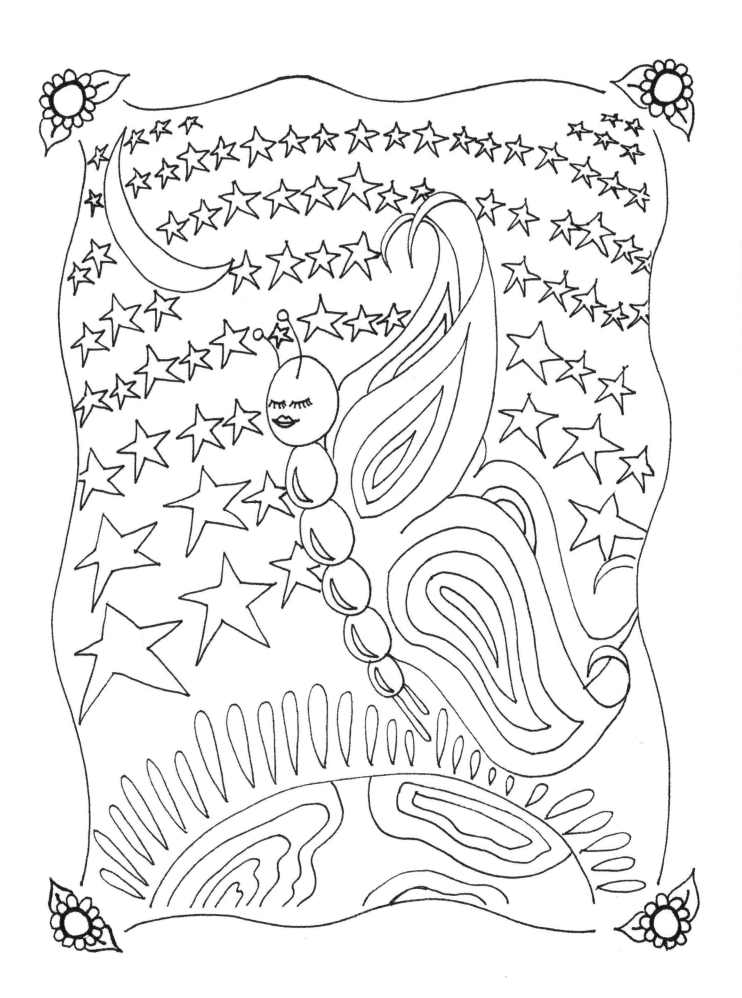

54308423R00081

Made in the USA
San Bernardino, CA
13 October 2017

Building Bridges
of Hope

Sue and Chelsea Badeau

Helping Hands Press

ISBN-13: 978-1-62208-593-4